Financial Literacy For Young Adults Amplified

Prepare for Inflation & Recession, Decide Between Buying or Renting, & Borrow Smarter

Raman Keane

Table of Contents

Introduction

"Formal education will make you a living; self-education will make you a fortune." ~ Jim Rohn

Imagine yourself getting on a roller coaster—the rush of adrenaline, sweaty palms, and a mix of fear and excitement as the ride begins. You have those times when you're feeling incredible, and then those moments when you're like, "What was I thinking?"

Roller coasters oddly resemble life in many ways. After all, there are ups and downs and scary moments that can also be exciting. Do you know what else is scary and exciting? Money and the economy.

Remember when you got your first paycheck? For me, it was thrilling and freeing. I felt so independent. But, with this joy, there is also fear attached to money. No one wants to lose it through poor decisions. When you decide to purchase your first home, you may experience a range of emotions. Not only are you excited and trying to remain confident, but also nervous and timid. There is something on the line.

Those thrills, twists, and turns of emotions sound like a roller coaster to me!

The big question is: Would you ever go on a roller coaster if you looked at the ride and it was strange or unsafe? If you went to the park and saw that it wasn't turning properly or had been in the news because of an accident. Would you still join a line to ride? Honestly, few people would dare to take the risk. You'd likely choose not to go to protect yourself.

If life and the economy are a roller coaster, you must feel confident about taking the ride. Not only should you be prepared for the twists and turns,

1

but you also need to assess whether the ride is safe. Are you starting to see the connection?

A study by Georgetown University estimated that the median earning of a person in the United States was about $1.7 million over a lifetime (Carnevale et al., n.d.). This number is probably even higher today. However, many people will agonize over spending a few hundred dollars on a new purchase rather than considering their long-term financial health. Furthermore, we often neglect the overall condition of our country's economy. It's like ignoring the rollercoaster's flaws and hopping on with no safety measures.

This is often because long-term finance is overwhelming. Where do you even start?

In my previous book, "Financial Literacy for Young Adults Simplified," I covered the fundamentals of finances. These fundamentals include money management, correct mindset, investing, cryptocurrencies, and retirement for beginners. Now, it is time to step up and broaden our perspective.

Our prolonged financial health depends on understanding the economy and money. But why should we study money beyond the fundamentals if we can handle it easily in our everyday lives? We can already earn, save, and spend it, so why invest more time in additional education?

Aristotle once said, "The educated differ from the uneducated as much as the living from the dead." This quote truly applies to various aspects of life, not just finances.

When I decided to purchase my first brand-new car, I was completely unaware of several crucial factors to consider when buying a vehicle. While I knew how to drive, had an excellent driving record, and could maintain my car, none of these skills helped me become a good car buyer. I ended up listening to a friend for recommendations. He chose a specific model, and I knew nothing of it except for his "wise" words. So, what was the problem? Well, the car was a perfect choice for my friend, but not for me.

This silly example isn't catastrophic or the worst thing that can happen when you aren't educated. However, imagine if I had applied the same method to other important financial decisions. I could have been in serious trouble.

Knowing how to budget, invest, and manage debt is like knowing how to operate a car. If you aim to make wise decisions during critical times, you need to know more than the basics. This is where learning financial concepts like inflation, recessions, interest rates, and borrowing comes into play.

Understanding these concepts helps us develop a roadmap highlighting potential traps in the future. If you know where these traps are, you can avoid falling into them. You can even arrange a detour to safely reach your destination.

The good news is that you aren't alone in this financial journey.

This book will give you the knowledge to create your roadmap. To do this, we'll cover topics like inflation and deflation and how they affect us. We'll also review methods for defending ourselves during economic downturns, such as recessions. Another concept we will dive into is the Federal Reserve and its impact on our lives.

We'll also touch on various types of loans and mortgages and compare renting vs. homeownership. Finally, we learn to make sense of the financial news and go through some breaking news together! The goal is to make these topics easier to understand by organizing them into manageable sections and explaining complicated terms and subjects.

Why these topics? Because they are closely related. As part of the economy, in the role of consumer or producer, we all feel their impact. For example, high inflation may cause the Fed to raise interest rates, which might cause the economy to fall into recession or deflation. These circumstances impact employment, mortgage rates, rents, and the entire economy, affecting our daily lives.

According to debt.org, in 2022, those aged 18 to 29 had an average non-mortgage debt of $12,871. This number more than doubled to an average of $26,532 for the 30 to 39 age group. Sadly, we rarely notice these trends in our financial lives and fail to take preventive measures, such as becoming financially literate.

You have taken the first step to avoid this fate. Now, all that's left is to work through the chapters as they cover topics that can affect your financial future.

Are you ready to start your journey to an amplified financial literacy?

Chapter 1

The Invisible Thief: Inflation

---•---

"Inflation is taxation without legislation." ~ Milton Friedman

One of the most unpleasant feelings is the sudden realization of how high the grocery bill has become or how expensive it is to enjoy a simple movie night. Prices are always fluctuating, and unfortunately, most of the time, they go up instead of down. When prices are rising dramatically, we hear the term inflation a lot. For example, after the COVID-19 pandemic, the economy saw a huge jump in prices, and news outlets started talking about inflation 24/7. For someone who is not familiar with inflation, this can be confusing and scary.

Technically speaking, inflation is not just a one-off phenomenon. It is always happening, but usually in a more controlled manner. Therefore, nobody talks about it, as it often goes unnoticed. Understanding inflation can really help you make better financial choices, especially for your long-term goals. So, let's take a deeper dive and see what inflation is and what we can do to deal with it.

The Rising Tide: What is Inflation?

In simple terms, inflation measures changes in the prices of goods and services over time. For example, last year, you may have paid $2 for a loaf of bread, but today it may cost $2.50. The loaf hasn't changed size or ingredients, and yet the price has increased.

Inflation is rarely as dramatic as the example above and instead acts like a rising tide. You may not notice a few cents here and there, but over time, it affects your overall cost of living.

The CPI

One of the key metrics used to calculate inflation is the Consumer Price Index (CPI). Using this index, the Bureau of Labor Statistics (BLS) tracks the average price changes of goods and services bought in a typical household.

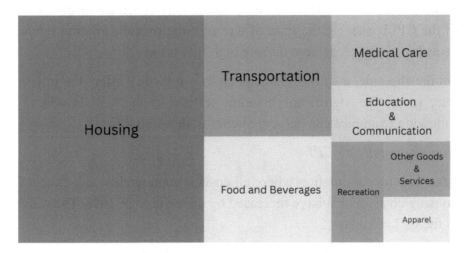

Figure 1.1 *Main categories in CPI. Each category may include multiple other subcategories.*

There are various categories within this index, with each assigned a different weight based on its impact on household expenses. These weight percentages change year after year according to consumer behaviors. For example, at the time of writing this book, food and beverages are a significant category, accounting for approximately 14% of the CPI "basket." This includes food inside the home (groceries) and outside the home (eating out at restaurants, cafes, etc.). On the other hand, housing makes up around 44% of the CPI basket, the largest category.

Some other CPI categories are transportation, recreation, apparel, etc. (see Figure 1.1). Each category may also have several subcategories.

The overall CPI is determined by calculating a weighted average. Essentially, this means that while some products or services may increase by 50 percent if they only account for a small percentage of the CPI, the overall rate of inflation won't see a dramatic increase.

A good example of this is gasoline. Gasoline prices can be extremely volatile. There have been occasions where gas prices increased by as much as 50 percent. However, as gasoline only accounts for around 4% of the CPI basket (at the time of writing), the overall inflation rate can be as low as 2 or 3 percent despite high fuel prices.

On the flip side, a shift in housing costs can swiftly affect the inflation rate, given the significant housing weight in the CPI basket. The following examples can help you better understand this.

Housing Impact on CPI:

Let's consider a situation where all costs remain unchanged, except for housing costs, which have increased by an average of 10%. The change in the CPI would be:

Increase in CPI=10% (change of housing costs) × 44% (the impact of housing on CPI) =

0.10×0.44 =

0.044 or **4.4%**

Gasoline Impact on CPI:

For the second example, let's imagine all prices remained the same except for gasoline, which has also increased by 10% from last year.

The increase in CPI $= 10\% \times 4\% =$

$0.10 \times 0.04 =$

0.004 or **0.4%**

We can clearly see that although both gasoline and housing had a 10% increase, the CPI increase was more significant in the first scenario compared with the second one. To learn more about different categories of the CPI and updated numbers, you can check the bls.gov portal.

The Impact of Inflation

According to the BLS, the U.S. average annual inflation rate over the last 20 years has been approximately 2.2%. In some years, though, inflation rates have been lower; in others, like the post-pandemic period, they were higher. (see Figure 1.2)

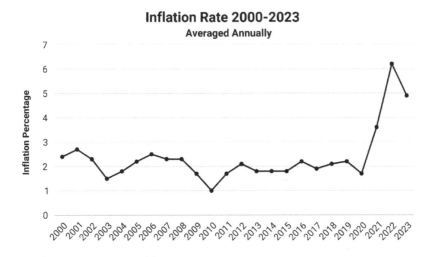

Figure 1.2 Average annual inflation rate from 2000 to October 2023

Source: (U.S. Bureau of Labor Statistics, 2023)

It is important to note that while no one enjoys paying more, inflation is not necessarily bad. The presence of moderate inflation (typically around

2%) suggests a healthy, growing economy. The keyword is moderate.

A thriving economy creates an environment where businesses can be more profitable. As a result, companies can also increase their employee's wages. Consequently, individuals find themselves with more money to spend. This increased spending can cause higher prices or rising inflation.

However, when there is too much inflation, it can be detrimental to the economy as a whole. Higher inflation erodes our purchasing power, making it more difficult for everyone, from individuals to big companies.

Imagine that you have spent the last year saving up for a new iPhone. You finally have the $1,000 you need, only to find that prices have increased by 20%. Now, you are short by at least $200. You can either stick with your old phone or use savings to purchase the new iPhone. In simple terms, if your income doesn't keep up with inflation, you're continuously getting poorer.

Despite having a paycheck that can cover rising expenses, there's still some uncertainty. Inflation can have a detrimental impact on your savings. This typically occurs when the rate of inflation is higher than the interest rate on your savings account. For example, if your bank offers 1% interest on your savings, but the inflation rate is 2%, your savings lose its value by at least 1%.

This creates an issue for savers since the value of their money is diminishing. Therefore, you need to choose your savings plan carefully to minimize the impact of inflation. Before opening a savings account, make sure to compare offerings from different banks.

The increase in prices not only affects shoppers but also businesses. When the cost of raw materials is higher, businesses need to either charge more or streamline their costs. This means that employees are unlikely to get raises, and in a worst-case scenario, they may suffer from layoffs.

If rising inflation is not addressed, it can lead to hyperinflation. This happens when prices rise significantly and continue to increase rapidly.

According to the World Bank, countries such as Venezuela and Zimbabwe have experienced hyperinflation. In such scenarios, countries typically face challenges like famine, failing financial institutions, and a loss of confidence in the government.

So, there is a fine balance between a healthy level of inflation that encourages business growth and financial instability.

Behind the Scenes: Causes of Inflation

Since the level of inflation is crucial to the health of an economy, it is important to understand the causes of inflation. These causes are often behind the scenes and driven by three key factors: demand-pull, cost-push, and built-in.

Demand-Pull

One of the primary reasons for inflation is when the demand for goods and services exceeds the existing supply. For instance, if every person who owns a mobile phone decides to upgrade to the newest model of the iPhone, Apple might struggle to meet the high demand, resulting in a potential price increase.

While higher iPhone prices may disappoint fans, their impact on the economy and inflation is limited. So, we need to factor in the larger perspective. The important question is why the demand for a broader range of goods and services in an economy could increase.

Several reasons influence demand levels. Some are straightforward, like population growth and optimism for the future when unemployment is low, and job security is high. However, other factors may require further explanation, such as the following:

Increased money supply: When the government applies stimulating policies, it can significantly influence how much money people or businesses have (see Chapter 4). As a result, they become more willing to invest or spend that additional money. This added spending can create supply constraints and drive up prices.

In the early days of the COVID-19 pandemic, businesses were shut down, and the economy went into recession. To offset this, the government tried to boost the economy with tools such as providing stimulus checks. U.S. personal savings surged during this time as people spent less and saved more of their income. Once the situation stabilized and things returned to normal, people started to spend these savings on a larger scale, causing a high demand for various goods and services (see Figure 1.3). Although other causes, like supply chain issues, contributed to higher inflation, the increased money supply played a significant role.

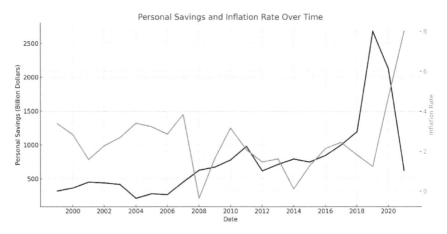

Figure 1.3 *Personal Savings (darker line) vs Inflation Rate (lighter line) in the U.S.*

Source: (Personal Saving Rate, 2024)

Depreciation of currency

When a nation's currency loses value, its products and services become cheaper for international buyers. Therefore, export demand increases as they become more attractive and affordable to global markets (Pettinger, 2020).

For example, if the value of the U.S. dollar drops, Europeans can buy American products at a lower price, resulting in increased purchases from Europe. The heightened demand for U.S. goods can drive up prices at home.

Cost-Push

Cost-push inflation occurs when raw materials or other production costs increase. As a result, companies must raise prices in order to protect their profit margins.

A prime example is the increase in oil prices. Oil is a key element for various industries, serving a vital role in transportation, manufacturing, and production. When oil prices spike, it has a domino effect on the economy.

Built-In

Built-in inflation occurs when businesses and workers expect prices to keep rising, leading to a continuous cycle of wage increases and price hikes (Frankel, 2024). For example, if the economy faces elevated inflation, employees across various industries may demand higher wages to cope with the rising cost of living. In response, businesses raise prices for their products or services to cover the higher wages, further exacerbating inflation.

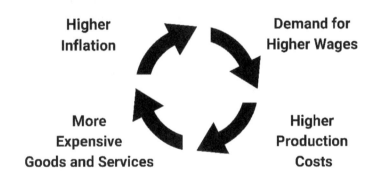

Higher Inflation

Demand for Higher Wages

More Expensive Goods and Services

Higher Production Costs

Figure 1.4 The cycle of built-in inflation.

Tackling Inflation

Although we can't control the inflation rate, we can still confront it effectively. It's important to plan for high inflation instead of waiting for it to happen. That's why learning about it as soon as possible is crucial.

Stay informed

It is easy to assume that inflation will take care of itself and bury our heads in the sand, but this is counterproductive. By staying on top of the current economic trends and government policies, you can make informed decisions to mitigate any effects of inflation.

To elaborate on this strategy, let's assume we regularly follow the economic news and learn that inflation has exceeded the regular 2-3% range. This might signal that the Federal Reserve will likely increase interest rates to combat inflation (more on this in upcoming chapters). Now, if we have a variable-rate mortgage, this interest hike can affect our monthly payment. We can mitigate this issue by converting the mortgage to a fixed rate or exploring more affordable housing options.

Budget Accordingly

When inflation is on the rise, you're going to see a change in your bank statements and receipts. So, it is important to budget for these changes. There is no point in sticking to your belief that you will spend $50 a week on groceries, and it will cover all of your items if prices have already started to increase. You will either need to swap to other, more budget-friendly items and reduce your shopping costs or adjust your budget.

If the inflation rate continues to increase, you will need to revisit your budget regularly to track your expenses.

Invest Wisely

If you have money to invest, you must invest wisely to combat inflation. Try looking into investments that typically outpace inflation. As mentioned earlier, basic savings accounts and similar products typically have interest rates lower than inflation, so you'll have to explore other options for your savings.

It is important to remember, though, that we can't wait to start investing until we experience high inflation. Considering inflation in our investment decisions, regardless of the current rate, is always a good idea. Remember, inflation is constantly changing. It doesn't go away.

Your investing options may include the following:

The Stock Market: While the returns you can expect from the stock market will depend on what you choose to invest in and how long you hold your assets, typically, the stock market can outpace inflation.

The S&P 500 is generally considered to represent a broad segment of the U.S. stock market, and between 1957 and 2023, it delivered an average annual return of 10.26% (Maverick, 2024). This doesn't mean you can expect this level of return every year, but it can give you an idea of the long term.

Also, bear in mind that a sudden inflation spike can cause market uncertainty, leading to stock values dropping in the short term.

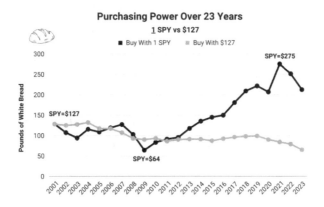

Figure 1.5 *Purchasing power of SPY vs. U.S. dollar in terms of buying pounds of bread.*

Sources: (SPY Stock Historical) & (BLS Data Viewer, n.d.)

The darker line in Figure 1.5 shows the average closing price of SPY for the month of May. SPY follows the movements of the S&P 500 Index.

Imagine you buy a share of SPY in 2001 for $127 and also save $127 in your savings account that pays almost zero interest. The price of bread continues to rise generally every year, so with the $127 cash you saved, you can buy less bread each year (the light gray line). However, with SPY in the long term, you can see that purchasing power increases (for simplicity, we didn't factor in potential capital gains tax).

I want to highlight the importance of the "Long Term" because, as you can see from the darker line, there were years when the stock market experienced negative returns. This is why we always need a diversified portfolio of cash and other assets to have options in different financial situations.

Real Assets: Tangible assets such as gold, silver, and other commodities or real estate tend to perform well even during high inflation.

TIPS and Bonds: TIPS (Treasury Inflation Protected Securities) are a type of government bond created to protect against inflation. When there are changes in the CPI, the government will adjust the principal value of the bond.

Essentially, with a bond, you are loaning money to a company, corporation, or government at an agreed rate for an agreed amount of time. This means that you know in advance how long you will hold the bond and what return you will receive at the end of the term. While certain bonds may not be viable options during high inflation, others can be quite attractive.

With TIPS, let's say you purchased $1000 worth of a 5-year bond that yields an interest of 1%. If the inflation rate reaches 2% in the first year, your interest will be calculated based on $1020 instead of $1000. Simply put, the principal is adjusted by the inflation rate.

Final Thoughts

Inflation is a complex phenomenon that can affect every aspect of our daily lives, from the prices we pay for groceries to the value of our savings and investments. By keeping ourselves informed about inflation trends and what drives them, we can make wiser financial decisions and plan for the future more effectively.

Chapter 2

The Downward Spiral:

Deflation

"The real problem is deflation. That is the opposite of inflation but equally serious to the borrower." ~ Jack Kemp

If inflation is bad, then logically reversing it should be good, correct? Well, It's more complicated than that. Think about it like blood pressure. Hypertension can be harmful, but low blood pressure can also have damaging effects. When it comes to the economy, we can compare hypertension to rising inflation and low blood pressure to deflation. In the upcoming sections, we will analyze deflation and discuss its common effects.

Understanding the Basics of Deflation

Deflation is a phenomenon that occurs when the prices of goods and services fall across the economic landscape for long enough to be considered a trend.

Unlike inflation, where your dollars allow you to buy less over time, during periods of deflation, your dollar can buy more. This can lead to economic stagnation, which means the economy struggles to grow.

Causes and Consequences

Deflation is primarily a result of two factors: lower demand or increased supply without a corresponding increase in demand. For example, the COVID-19 pandemic caused a sharp decline in air travel demand and a 33% decrease in fares in business-focused markets in 2020 (Stalnaker et al., n.d.). Of course, there are other reasons for changes in demand or supply that are more frequently seen. Here are a few of the causes and effects.

Reduced consumer spending

Economic downturns, like recessions, can lead to a decrease in overall consumer spending. One example is that people tend to have a more negative outlook on the economy's future during a recession. Therefore, they hold on to their big purchases and try to save more money instead (see Chapter 3). This ultimately results in reduced consumer demand.

Reduced Money Supply

Central bank policies like increasing interest rates can affect the money supply in the economy (see Chapter 4). For example, a high interest rate may hinder people from borrowing and spending money, consequently reducing product and service sales.

Reduced Production Cost

If the price of essential materials like oil decreases, it can reduce the production costs. As a result, companies may attempt to boost their production, potentially leading to an excess supply in the market.

The same phenomenon can occur because of technological advancements. Using new technologies can reduce production costs and trigger an uptick in production.

Unfortunately, deflation can develop into a vicious cycle of ever-decreasing spending. When prices fall, people typically avoid spending now, anticipating lower prices later. This leads to less demand, prompting companies to reduce prices further.

How Does Deflation Impact You?

During deflation, prices decrease, allowing for increased purchasing power, but various consequences can exist. Some of these effects consist of the following:

Job and Wage Uncertainty

During deflation, your costs may decrease, and you can buy more with your paycheck. However, you could face job and wage uncertainty. If your employer needs to cut the prices of the company's products or services to compete in the marketplace, they may be forced to make salary cuts, reduce their hours, or, in a worst-case scenario, lay off some staff. Additionally, if the period of deflation leads to instability throughout the economy, there could be greater job insecurities. Even freelancers and the self-employed can feel the impact of deflation. Clients may see the prices of other goods and services dropping and be unwilling to pay your current rates.

Deflation Can Affect Your Debts

If you have borrowed money, deflation can make your debt more costly in real terms. Let's say, for instance, that you took out a car loan for $10,000. If the economy enters a period of deflation, you will continue to owe this sum. However, as we mentioned, you may receive less monthly income.

Moreover, if the prices decrease, the value of your purchased car could be much lower than $10,000, resulting in a situation where you owe more than the car is worth. In fact, you may even find that the price of new models is less than the money you owe on your older vehicle.

Deflation Can Influence Your Savings

When the economy experiences deflation, the relative value of savings increases since your money can buy more. Unfortunately, deflation and economic instability often go hand in hand, so your income may be at risk, or you may have concerns about your job security.

Let's think about this in terms of buying power. If you want to purchase a new laptop during a deflationary period, you can buy a better model with the same sum of money. But whether you pay outright or finance your purchase, better buying power will only benefit you if you can rely on the stability of your income. If you have concerns that you may experience a salary cut or lose your job, you may need to dip into your savings to cover your everyday costs. If you've spent that money upfront on a computer, it's gone, and selling it may not recover your costs.

Avoiding or Mitigating the Negative Impacts of Deflation

It should now be clear that deflation can be potentially as harmful to your finances as inflation. Fortunately, there are some ways you can begin to deflation-proof your budget and expenses.

The Do's and Don'ts of Deflation

DO pay off debts: As discussed earlier, any debt will be immediately more expensive during deflationary periods. Therefore, paying off as many of your outstanding debts as possible is important. Obviously, carrying debt is not the best spending strategy in most circumstances, but when the purchasing power of money is rising, you want to avoid owing more than absolutely necessary.

DON'T borrow with your credit cards: Continuing the previous point, if the economy is entering a phase of deflation, keep those credit cards locked up tight. Even 'small' purchases can accumulate on your credit card balance and end up costing you more in the long run. Pay your credit balance in full or simply pay with cash or a debit card.

DON'T Let Deflation Derail Your Portfolio: When there is a risk of deflation, investors usually shift their focus to defensive investments like high-quality bonds, as they tend to perform better. Companies that produce essential consumer goods, like food, drugs, and toiletries, are considered defensive stocks. While stocks that offer dividends are also favored, it is critical to choose ones from reputable companies with a reliable history of dividend payments (Smith, 2022).

DO keep cash on hand: Unlike periods of inflation, keeping cash on hand during deflation can be a good idea. Since the real-term value of your money increases, having cash on hand can allow you to take advantage of any good deals when they appear. As discussed in the previous chapter, it's wise to keep your extra cash in an account that earns interest, like a high-yield savings account. However, whether you decide to save or invest, the crucial aspect is to ensure easy liquidity.

The Lifeline of Liquidity

Let's discuss liquidity, which you saw mentioned in the last section. To put it simply, liquidity measures how easily assets can be converted to cash. And when we talk about how liquid an asset is, cash is always number one on the list, which looks like this:

1. Cash

2. Cash banked in checking or savings accounts

3. Gold, silver, and other precious metals commodities

4. Securities like stocks or mutual funds

5. Accounts receivable: people paying their outstanding debt to you

6. Inventory: selling items you have in stock. (e.g., the inventory of your store)

7. Fixed assets: big-ticket items like real estate, equipment, and vehicles

For example, money in a checking account is more liquid than gold, even though gold can and does sell quickly. Why? Because you can go to your bank yourself and withdraw your funds. When you sell gold, you must factor in the extra time and expense of going through a gold dealer.

Having access to liquid assets can provide a real lifeline. In a financial emergency, you might be unable to get hold of cash and may be forced to rely on credit cards or financing to cover your expenses. That's why it's so important to have an emergency fund of cash or other easily liquidated assets set aside for a crisis, or as some people like to call it, a rainy day. Most experts recommend having three to six months of your typical monthly expenses in your emergency fund, but even having an emergency fund equivalent to one month of your expenses is better than nothing.

Strategizing for Liquidity

You can employ several strategies to ensure that you have easy access to your emergency fund. A basic savings account is a standard option but may not provide optimal returns. While it is possible to invest in higher-paying assets, this could compromise the liquidity of your emergency fund. The challenge is to find investment products that offer good returns and are easy to liquidate.

An excellent example is a high-yield savings account, which may limit the number of times you can withdraw money each month but offers far higher interest rates than a standard savings account. You could also take advantage of short-term CDs. Even though these options don't provide the highest rates, you'll experience a shorter delay when you need to access your funds.

Ask yourself, "How long can I afford to wait for my cash?" This helps you understand what type of delay you can live with and strategize where to put your money. If you can't wait at all, then cash is the optimal choice. If you are able to wait for a week, a month, or even longer, you can start exploring assets or investments that offer greater long-term value but have less immediate liquidity. Be aware that you should never tie up all your assets in investments with limited liquidity, especially when deflation threatens to destabilize the economy.

The bottom line on liquidity is to be smart and, if you're able, keep a good mix of lower-return, higher-liquid assets AND higher-return, lower-liquid assets. If you don't have enough money or credit to diversify your investments, be sure that what you have is as liquid as possible to safeguard your financial stability.

Final Thoughts

On the surface, deflation feels like a blessing because it puts money back into our pockets by giving each dollar greater buying power. But buying power isn't everything, and by knowing what steps to take or not to take, you can keep more of your money and remain financially stable during uncertain economic times. The next chapter will delve into recession, another significant economic phenomenon.

Chapter 3

Riding the Economic

Roller Coaster: Recession

———————

"Unfortunately, in a recession, the people who suffer the most aren't the rich but the wanna-be rich and the poor." ~ Robert Kiyosaki

You've probably heard of the "recession" on the news or from people who went through it. People often speak about recession in dire terms, with experts predicting severe issues for all consumers. However, when you can grasp the nature of recessions, you can equip yourself to navigate these potential challenges and make informed decisions even during an economic downturn. In this chapter, we'll help you understand recessions so you can ride this economic roller coaster more comfortably.

The Nature of Recessions

As touched upon in previous chapters, a slowed-down economy can indicate an impending recession. But what is a recession? A recession is defined as a period of significant decline in economic activity (House, 2022). The general rule of thumb is that a recession constitutes two consecutive quarters with a negative GDP (Gross Domestic Product) growth. However, the National Bureau of Economic Research (NBER), the official entity for tracking recessions, considers various factors before determining if the economy is in a recession.

The severity of economic decline can vary in recessions. An excellent example of a mild recession is the 2001 bursting of the dot-com bubble. Because internet-based companies, like Pets.com and others, experienced rapid, unsustainable growth, it caused a temporary, unstable boost to the economy. When the bubble burst, these business models collapsed, triggering a mild recession and significant economic impact. The NASDAQ Composite, a stock market index that is heavy with tech companies, lost a massive 78 percent of its value between its peak in March 2000 and bottom in October 2002.

During the 2020 pandemic, the NBER determined that the economy entered a recession. This happened because businesses were forced to close, and people stayed home due to health concerns. Consumers were not spending money in stores, restaurants, and entertainment venues, resulting in several quarters of negative economic growth.

Although this may sound like a worrisome situation, it is important to remember that recessions are part of the economic cycle and are typically followed by a period of recovery. Sometimes, we can even go from a recession to a booming economy. Therefore, we just need to be prepared to weather the storm.

The 2008 recession was so devastating that it is often referred to as the Great Recession. The housing market went from a boom to a severe decline. When the housing bubble burst, many people ended up with expensive mortgages with balances higher than their property values, known as being upside down on their loans or having negative equity. Homeowners were not the only ones affected; financial institutions that held a significant number of mortgage-backed securities also faced difficulties.

The collapse caused a domino effect that troubled many banks. As a result, the government had to step in and rescue them from disaster. They used $245 billion of taxpayer funds (Bennett, 2023) as part of the Troubled Asset Relief Program (TARP) to stabilize these financial institutions and prevent total economic collapse. This massive bailout triggered changes to regulatory, monetary, and fiscal federal policies that remain in effect today.

Although devastating, a long period of U.S. economic growth followed the 2008 Great Recession. Unemployment dropped from 10% in October 2009 to 3.5% in February 2020, just before the COVID-19 pandemic.

Recession's Ripple Effects

When a recession hits, it can have a ripple effect across various sectors of the economy. One of the most significant effects of a recession is its impact on the job market. When economic times become tougher, companies often look to streamline their costs to remain profitable. This leads to layoffs, job-cutting, and higher unemployment rates (Figure 3.1). Many businesses suffered and shuttered their doors because of the 2008 recession. From smaller businesses up to giants such as Lehman Brothers, who had mass layoffs, it created an enormous spike in unemployment.

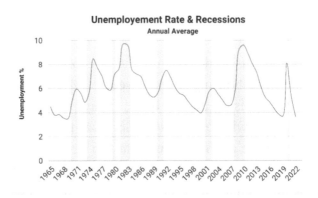

Figure 3.1 Gray areas show the approximate period of recession

Source: (Unemployment Rate, 2024).

During a recession, younger adults may find it challenging to enter the job market or move to more senior positions. This is because companies are more cautious and hire less. Since graduating classes happen regardless of what is going on in the economy, a recession can potentially leave thousands of young adults struggling to enter the workforce.

Companies being more frugal can also affect wages and salary growth. It's not uncommon for companies to implement pay freezes or even cut salaries to save on their costs. When businesses face the need to cut costs, employee compensation and benefits are typically the first areas to be affected.

If you've recently graduated and have entered the workforce, you may struggle to see a salary higher than the base rate for several years. You may have purposely taken an entry-level position after graduating in anticipation of gaining experience and the associated higher wage, but, unfortunately, during a recession, you may struggle to see this pay increase.

A 2011 study conducted by the Economic Policy Institute (Bell & Blanchflower, 2011) also supported this theory. The research team found workers who graduate during a recession earn less for approximately 15 years after entering the workforce.

Reduced hiring forces graduates into more entry-level positions or even unrelated fields with lower salaries. For instance, if you graduate with the intention of a marketing career, you may end up working in administration, food services, or retail while you wait for marketing companies to begin rehiring.

Hiring freezes like this also tend to have a trickle-down effect from industry to industry. Fewer manufacturing jobs mean fewer raw materials needed, so material handling jobs will also diminish, as will the logistics and transportation jobs required to move raw and finished materials.

Recessions and Your Wallet

Recessions not only affect the employment prospects but also the personal finances, particularly borrowing and spending patterns. All companies, including financial institutions, tend to be more cautious during a recession. You may struggle to qualify for even basic financing, such as a credit card or personal loan. During the 2008 recession, banks tightened their lending standards across the board. This made it harder for people to get credit. Even if you had an excellent credit rating, getting a home loan or other financing was extremely difficult.

However, the central banks often try to stimulate economic activity during a recession by lowering the base interest rate. This cascades throughout the economy as interest rates on borrowing and savings decrease (see Chapter 4). That's a *good* thing if you have a secure income and good credit score because it can be a great time to lock in a low fixed-rate loan to borrow for a big-ticket item, such as a home. However, there are two key points you should consider.

- During recessions, it is not recommended to opt for adjustable-rate loans (see Chapter 7) as their rates may rise after the recovery phase.

- Additionally, don't take your job for granted; always have a backup plan, such as emergency funds, for loan repayments in case of job loss.

Recessions can also have a massive impact on the housing market. Since borrowing can be more challenging and job security can be a little shaky, many people postpone moving home. After all, if you are considering purchasing a new home but are not 100 percent certain about your income, you may not want to commit to a new mortgage and the expenses of buying property. Many people who have considered upgrading to a new home may choose to stay put and possibly make improvements to remain comfortable in their existing home.

Some homeowners may find themselves in a situation of negative equity, where the value of their home is less than the amount outstanding on their home loan. This means they are stuck with their existing home, even if they want to move. This results in fewer buyers within the housing market. Those who still want to sell their home will likely find fewer buyers showing interest and may have to drop their asking price to secure a sale.

In severe recessions, banks may repossess and sell borrowers' homes who are struggling with their mortgage payments. This creates another opportunity for new buyers to spend less when buying from a bank.

The reduced demand sends property prices plunging across most markets. According to CoreLogic, home prices in the U.S. dropped by 19.7 percent during the Great Recession (Team, 2023).

While this is bad news for homeowners, it potentially presents new opportunities for first-time buyers. You may have a stronger bargaining position and may be able to negotiate an extremely good deal on your first home, provided you can secure a mortgage.

Staying Afloat in a Recession

As you can see, a recession doesn't need to be all doom and gloom—there are some ways that help you not only stay afloat but benefit from reduced economic activity.

Consider these factors:

Having an Emergency Fund

An emergency fund is crucial, yet many people are unprepared. In a Bank of America report, the researchers discovered that 71 percent of millennials don't have a three-month emergency fund (Gillespie, 2023). This lack of financial planning means they have no financial fallback in an emergency and may rely on credit cards or other expensive forms of borrowing.

Cutting Back on Non-Essential Spending

Being able to stretch your finances when there is a downturn in the economy can be very helpful. It would be best to cut back on your non-essential spending to achieve this. Take some time to go through your bank statements and credit cards to highlight any non-essential spending. Of course, you'll still need to pay your rent, utilities, and other necessary costs, but you may be able to trim some of your other expenses.

Boosting Your Skills and Qualifications

When the job market is going through a tough patch, boosting your skills and qualifications can make you marketable to potential employers. You can take online courses on almost everything from coding to marketing to keep your skills up to date. If you lack experience, consider volunteering or taking on an internship to build your skill set. If you're graduating during a recession or have recently graduated when the economy is heading for a downturn, remember the job market will be highly competitive—you need to stand out from the crowd. The best way to do this is with a resume packed with skills, qualifications, and experience.

Making Sure Your Credit Score is High

We've already discussed how a recession can provide an opportunity for first-time buyers and young adults to secure financing. However, since banks are more cautious during a recession, you'll need a high credit score to qualify. Check your current score and see if there is anything you can do to ensure your score is as high as possible (see Chapter 5).

Don't Go Over Your Risk Tolerance

If you are investing your excess cash, avoid going over your risk tolerance and overestimating your limits. While trying for the greatest possible returns might be tempting, these often come with the highest risks. Remember that a recession can affect various investment options, and returns are not guaranteed. Stick to lower-risk options unless you have a great deal of investing experience and a keen awareness of the risks of different investment strategies.

Staying Informed About the Economy

You don't have to subscribe to every financial publication immediately, but staying informed about the economy and financial markets is crucial. This will help you make wiser decisions during economic downturns (see Chapter 9).

Final Thoughts

The prospect of a recession can be intimidating, particularly if you don't fully grasp why it could be bad for you. However, once you understand how and why a recession occurs and what you can do to protect yourself, you can avoid making bad choices and premature reactions that could hurt you in the long run. We discussed how central banks respond during challenging times, such as recessions. The following chapter will explore the Federal Reserve and how it influences the economy.

Chapter 4

Decoding the Federal Reserve

———•———

"The process by which banks create money is so simple the mind is repelled. With something so important, a deeper mystery seems only decent."
~ John Kenneth Galbraith

Our nation's economy is like a gigantic machine with millions of moving parts. Within those moving parts, some are bigger, and some are smaller. One of the most significant pieces is the Federal Reserve. Despite being frequently mentioned, most people are unfamiliar with its true nature. At first glance, understanding the Federal Reserve system and its role seems like rocket science. However, once you understand it, you'll see why our economy works the way it does.

In this chapter, we are going to uncover the inner workings of the Federal Reserve machinery. We will examine its structure, the people in charge, and their management of the money supply. Ultimately, we will assess the effects of their decisions on our daily lives.

Introduction to the Federal Reserve

The Federal Reserve, commonly known as the "Fed," is the United States central bank (Federal Reserve System | USAGOV, n.d.). As a central bank, it is the "bank of banks," acting as the main stabilization gear of the U.S. economy. The Fed was created in 1913 and, since then, has been instrumental in responding to financial panics and recessions, such as the 1929 banking crisis that led to the Great Depression.

Contrary to what most people believe, the Fed is not a 100% government institution. It is somehow a hybrid organization, combining government-based regulations and private stockholders like commercial banks.

Twelve regional Federal Reserve banks are spread throughout the country as part of the Fed system. Every regional reserve bank has a corporation-like structure with a board of directors. The shareholders of the Reserve Banks are other banks and financial institutions (e.g., Bank of America), also known as Member Banks.

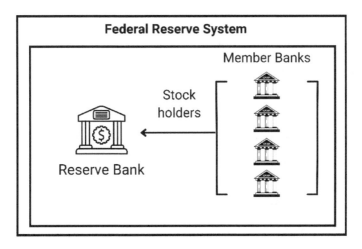

Figure 4.1 *The Federal Reserve is a system composed of twelve reserve banks, with member banks acting as shareholders.*

Treasury vs Fed

Before moving further with the Federal Reserve discussion, it is worth briefly touching on the key differences between the Fed and the Treasury, as they sometimes get confused. The Treasury focuses on the government's budget, whereas the Fed focuses on managing the overall economy and controls the broader money supply through interest rates and bank regulations.

The Fed has the power to issue U.S. dollars under the Federal Reserve Act of 1913. However, printing physical bills and minting coins are handled by agencies within the U.S. Treasury.

Creation of the Federal Reserve

In general, the Fed's creation was the response to a number of financial crises and the need for stability in the banking system. Since the United States didn't have a central bank to supervise other banks, the government felt the need to create one. By creating a central bank, the banking system would become more stable and less susceptible to panics, ensuring the economy's health and safeguarding the public's savings.

Let's take a look at the key points related to the Fed's creation:

- **Financial Panics:** In the 19th and early 20th centuries, the United States experienced many financial panics and banking crises. These crises often occurred due to the absence of a central authority to oversee banking activities, a fragmented banking system with numerous small banks issuing their own currency, and a lack of mechanisms to support banks with liquidity during challenging times.

- **Calls for Reform:** The recurring financial crises prompted calls for reform to establish a more stable banking system. Economists, policymakers, and bankers advocated creating a central bank to regulate the banking industry, provide a uniform currency, and serve as a safety net to prevent bank runs and financial panics. In the event of a bank run, a significant number of depositors lose faith in the bank and rush to withdraw their money at the same time. This can happen because of rumors, negative news, or a general sense of economic instability.

- **Legislative Efforts:** Several attempts were made to create a central bank in the United States prior to the establishment of the Federal Reserve. The First and Second Banks of the United States were early attempts, but both faced opposition and were eventually dissolved. In 1907, a severe financial panic known as the Panic of 1907 further underscored the need for banking reform.

- **Federal Reserve Act of 1913:** In response to the ongoing calls for banking reform and the lessons learned from the Panic of 1907, Congress passed the Federal Reserve Act in 1913. President Woodrow Wilson signed the act into law on December 23, 1913. The Federal Reserve Act created the Federal Reserve System as the primary banking authority in the U.S.

- **Key Provisions:** The Federal Reserve Act gave the Federal Reserve the authority to conduct monetary policy, regulate banks, provide financial services, and oversee the nation's payment systems (LabLynx, 2022).

The Structure of the Federal Reserve System

The structure of the Federal Reserve is decentralized and supported by a strong network. The main idea behind decentralization is to avoid having all control and authority in one place by distributing it. Each element within this network holds distinct roles and responsibilities.

The Fed has these three key parts:

- The Board of Governors
- The Regional Reserve Banks
- The Federal Open Market Committee (FOMC)

It's worth noting that while these components function independently, they don't run in isolation. As a result, each element contributes to the Fed's overall functions, but without one section interfering with another. So, let's look at what each main component does.

The Board of Governors

- The Board of Governors is like the big boss of the Federal Reserve System. It is located in Washington, D.C., and consists of seven members appointed by the President of the United States and confirmed by the Senate (Sharma, 2024).

- The members of the Board of Governors serve 14-year terms to maintain continuity and independence. The Chairman and Vice Chairman of the Board are chosen from the members and serve for four years.

- The Board of Governors is in charge of establishing monetary policy, overseeing and regulating banks, supervising the operations of the Federal Reserve Banks, and ensuring the financial system's stability.

The Regional Reserve Banks

- The Federal Reserve System is divided into twelve regional districts, each served by a Federal Reserve Bank. These banks are located in major cities across the country, like New York, San Francisco, Chicago, and Atlanta.

- Reserve Banks offer banking services to local banks, like check services, giving out cash, and making online payments.

- They also play a role in implementing monetary policy through participation in the FOMC. We'll get to that later.

Figure 4.2 shows the distribution of the twelve regional reserve banks across different regions of the United States.

Figure 4.2 *Federal Reserve's twelve Districts*

While each reserve bank has its own jurisdiction, it acts under decisions and policies enacted by the Board of Governors. They work with local financial institutions to implement specific actions within their jurisdiction.

Federal Open Market Committee (FOMC)

- The Federal Open Market Committee is in charge of making money decisions at the Federal Reserve System. The group consists of seven members from the Board of Governors, the President of the Reserve Bank of New York, and four of the remaining eleven Reserve Bank presidents, who take turns serving (Federal Reserve 2009).

- The FOMC meets regularly to assess economic conditions and review monetary policy options. They are responsible for making critical decisions, like setting interest rates.

The Federal Reserve's Role

The Federal Reserve typically becomes more visible when discussions about interest rates arise. It's also quite common to see the Fed Chairman discuss issues regarding the economy as a whole. However, the Fed's role is far greater than most people suppose. The Fed covers a wide range of topics related to our economy. That is why we will look at the Federal Reserve's role in greater detail.

Bank of Banks

The Federal Reserve Banks function as the banks of banks, offering financial services to depository institutions such as commercial banks. These services include:

- Maintains accounts for the regular banks and moves money between banks quickly and securely.

- Distributing physical currency to meet the public's demand for cash.

- Facilitating electronic money transfers and settlements through services like Fedwire.

- When a bank is running low on cash and can't borrow from other banks, the Federal Reserve steps in to help as a last resort.

Research

Economists within the Federal Reserve System contribute to:

- Conducting economic research and analysis to understand the functioning of the economy and financial markets.

- Providing insights into economic trends, inflation, employment, and other key factors influencing monetary policy decisions.

- Informing policymakers about the potential impact of various policy options and helping them make informed decisions.

- Enhancing public understanding of economic issues through publications, data releases, and public speeches.

Monetary Policy Implementation

The Federal Reserve employs Monetary Policy to control the money supply and promote economic growth. They have two goals to accomplish, also known as dual mandates:

1. Maximum Employment
2. Keeping Inflation in Check

The Federal Reserve implements monetary policy through various tools, which we'll explain soon. However, to understand them, we must first learn what security is, specifically treasury securities.

Treasury Securities

The national debt is always a hot topic for politicians, especially during elections. But have you ever wondered how the government gets into debt? Treasury securities are one of the tools they use to issue debt.

In simple terms, "security" is when investors invest their money in a business, expecting to profit from the efforts of others (What Is a Security?, n.d). For example, stocks are securities because you invest your money in a business by buying its stocks and expect to profit from it, even though other people run that business.

In the case of treasury securities, investors lend money to the government and expect to receive repayment with interest at a later time (Fernando, 2023). Because of the backing of the U.S. government's credit, they are often considered highly secure investments. Commercial banks hold large amounts of treasury securities as a part of their overall assets. Investors can also sell or buy these securities even before they mature.

There are three types of treasury securities based on when they mature:

- **Treasury bills (T-bills):** Short-term, ranging from 4 weeks to 52 weeks.

- **Treasury notes (T-notes):** Medium-term, ranging from 2 to 10 years.

- **Treasury bonds (T-bonds):** Long-term, 20 or 30 years.

Now that treasury securities are out of the way let's explore monetary policy and discover the Fed's primary tools for managing the money supply.

Open Market Operations (OMO)

This term is used when the Federal Reserve does any of the following:

- **Buys** the treasury securities from the banks and institutions. This helps banks have more money to lend because they've exchanged their securities for money. Consequently, the *Federal Fund Rate* goes down. This is the interest rate banks charge when they lend money to each other. A lower federal fund rate can potentially lower other interests that you and I use, like car loans and mortgage interest.

- **Sells** treasury securities to banks. Because of this, banks now have less money for lending since they've swapped it for securities. As a result, an increase in the federal fund rate potentially leads to higher interest rates for other loans.

Quantitative Easing (QE) and Tightening (QT)

This is similar to OMO, where easing refers to buying, and tightening refers to selling. The main difference is that in OMO, the focus is more on buying or selling short-term securities. In contrast, QE and QT tend to buy or sell more long-term securities and other assets, like mortgage securities, to affect the interest rate for a longer period.

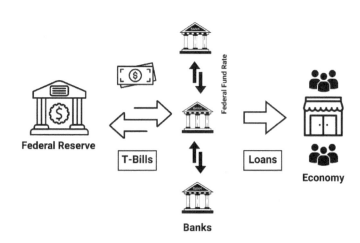

Figure 4.3 Expansionary Open Market Operation. The Fed Buys T-Bills from banks and increases their money supply.

Setting the Discount Rate

This is the interest rate at which banks borrow from the Federal Reserve. If the Federal Reserve raises the discount rate, banks will have to pay more to borrow money, which could lead to higher interest rates for the general public.

Reserve Requirements

The Fed mandates banks to keep a certain percentage of their total deposit in reserve. For example, if one bank holds $10 million in customers' deposits and the reserve requirement is 10%, it should keep $1 million in reserve all the time and can not lend it out. If they increase this percentage, banks will have less money to lend and can effectively raise the interest rate for the public.

Bank Supervision and Regulation

The Federal Reserve monitors banks to ensure their health and compliance with regulations, such as maintaining sufficient funds and safeguarding customers. They set the rules banks should follow. They also work with other agencies to ensure banks are doing things right and controlling risks.

The Fed's Magic Money Printer

We covered how the Fed affects the economy using different tools such as OMO, Discount Rate, etc. Let's unravel the most common remark about them: "The Fed is printing money!"

When people say that the Fed is printing money, they are basically referring to the processes we described earlier, which cause the money supply to increase. For example, as mentioned in the OMO section, the Fed can buy securities from banks and increase their money reserves.

But where does that money come from? The truth is, the Fed doesn't necessarily need to have that money on hand. They can simply credit the banks digitally, essentially creating new money (Ross, 2023). It's like having a bank account where you can change the balance without putting in any actual money.

While printing money by the Fed can boost the economy in the short term, if left unchecked, it can have significant negative effects, such as higher inflation and devaluation of the U.S. dollar (Agbaje, 2023).

The Impact of the Federal Reserve on the Economy

The Fed's actions directly affect our economy and, by extension, the world economy. Since the United States dollar is the world's reserve currency, every action or statement by the Fed will have a global impact. In particular, let's take a look at how the Fed's actions directly affect our economy:

Interest Rates

As mentioned earlier, the Fed controls our nation's monetary policy. They can stimulate or restrain economic activity by adjusting the federal funds rate and using other tools. For instance, the Fed raises interest rates when inflation rises beyond reasonable levels. In contrast, the Fed can slash interest rates to spur economic growth in times of recession. While interest rate decisions have a clear psychological impact on banks, investors, and the public, there are various ways in which these decisions affect our economy.

- **Consumer Loans and Mortgages:** Changes in interest rates set by the Federal Reserve can affect the rates consumers pay on loans such as mortgages, auto loans, and credit cards.

- **Business Investment:** Lower interest rates make borrowing money for equipment, facilities, and expansion projects cheaper, increasing business investment and economic growth. On the other hand, higher interest rates can raise the cost of borrowing for businesses, potentially slowing down investment and economic activity.

- **Savings and Investments:** The interest rates set by the Federal Reserve also affect the returns on savings and investments.

Lower rates may discourage saving in interest-bearing accounts but may encourage investment in riskier assets for higher returns. Higher rates may incentivize saving but could lead to lower returns on certain investments.

Experts and analysts always try to interpret the Fed's words to determine where interest rates will go. The aim is to get ahead of the trend to capitalize on price shifts. The stock market is also affected by the Fed's decision. Generally, when the Feds aim to lower interest rates, it's seen as a positive factor for the market. However, if they signal any tightening policies, the market usually reacts negatively.

Employment

The Fed does not play a direct role in employment, meaning it cannot decide on hiring, firing, wages, etc. Instead, the Fed's actions help create the conditions necessary to grow employment levels and maintain stable wages. Similarly, the Fed strives to protect wages by keeping inflation in check. Let's take a look at how these actions occur:

- **Employment and Economic Growth:** Decisions on interest rates and monetary policy can affect economic growth and employment levels. Lower interest rates can stimulate economic activity, leading to increased hiring by businesses and lower unemployment rates. Conversely, higher interest rates may slow down economic growth and lead to higher unemployment if businesses cut back on hiring and investments.

- **Inflation and Wage Growth:** The Federal Reserve monitors inflation closely as part of its mandate. Moderate inflation around 2% *(*Inflation of 2 percent *n.d.)* is generally viewed as conducive to a healthy economy. The Fed's actions to control inflation can indirectly influence wage growth and employment dynamics.

Final Thoughts

While you don't have to read every Federal Reserve report and analysis, staying informed about their actions is important. As you have noticed, their decisions can drastically influence our finances. From facing higher interest rates to potentially getting our employment affected. Ultimately, the greater our knowledge, the better prepared we become to confront uncertainties.

Chapter 5

Understanding Loans and

Borrowing Wisely

"A small debt produces a debtor; a large one, an enemy." ~
Publilius Syrus

Loans can feel like a financial burden. You have probably heard loan-related horror stories among your friends and family. News coverage may highlight families losing their homes because they couldn't meet their loan obligations. That is why it is imperative to expand our knowledge of loans.

Understanding Different Types of Loans

Knowing about different loan types is essential for making intelligent financial decisions, as each type has unique features, advantages, and requirements. However, it is important to understand the two terms commonly used in the lending industry.

Secured Loans: These are loans that are backed by an asset or collateral, which is something tangible that you pledge to get your loan. Collateral reduces the risk for the lender since they can take your assets to recover the outstanding funds if you fail to repay your loan. Typical examples are mortgages, where the property is used as collateral, and auto loans, where the vehicle is the asset.

Debt Consolidation: This is simply combining multiple debts into one loan. If you had two credit card accounts, a personal loan, and an auto loan, you could combine them into one. Generally, the consolidation loan offers better repayment terms or a lower interest rate. Moreover, it might be just easier to manage making one loan payment instead of several.

Let's now discuss the various types of loans.

Personal Loans: These loans don't require collateral because they are usually unsecured. Personal loans can be a good option for large purchases, debt consolidation, or unexpected bills. The interest rate for personal loans depends on your credit score, but generally, there are flexible repayment terms.

Auto Loans: These loans are specifically designed for vehicle purchases, and the loan uses the car as collateral. Since auto loans are secured, they often offer lower interest rates.

Student Loans: Student loans are the most appropriate type of funding for higher education and are available as federal or private funding. In either case, they cover expenses like tuition, books, etc. Federal student loans generally come with lower interest rates and more options for paying back. They may also offer greater protections.

Mortgages: These are long-term loans that are meant for buying a property, where the property itself is the collateral. Because of this security, mortgages offer lower interest rates. Your payment and interest rate depend on many factors, such as loan duration, interest rate type, etc. (see Chapter 7).

Home Equity Loan: These loans use the equity in your home as security for the loan, so they are a little more of an 'advanced' concept. You might want a home equity loan to renovate and increase your property's overall value. A home equity loan provides a lump sum at a fixed rate, but it's important to mention that, like a mortgage, your home is at risk if you default on repayment.

Payday Loans: These are short-term, high-cost loans, usually for $500 or less. Usually, they are expected to be paid on your next payday. Storefront lenders and online platforms may offer payday loans, depending on the laws in each state. Payday lending is unavailable in some states either because state laws prohibit it or because payday lenders have opted not to conduct business under those states' interest rate and fee guidelines (Payday Loan| Consumer Financial Protection Bureau, 2022).

Small Business Loans: If you are starting or expanding a small business, this is your loan type. Small business loans can come from various sources, including Small Business Administration (SBA) loans backed by the federal government. You can also look into bank loans, considering that all small business lenders have their own requirements to qualify.

Lines of Credit: This flexible loan option provides a set amount of funds you can draw from as you need. You only pay interest on the amount you use, but set-up and administrative fees may be associated with a line of credit. A line of credit can be a good option as an emergency fund if you have ongoing expenses.

As you can see, each type of loan has a distinct purpose and considerations to account for when you need to apply for funding.

Assessing Financial Readiness

Before you seriously consider taking on loan debt, you must assess your financial readiness. This involves evaluating your personal finances, implementing an adequate budget, and employing financial planning strategies. The following checklist is a great place to start with.

✔ **Check Your Credit Score:** The three major credit bureaus can provide a copy of your credit report. While we touched on credit scores briefly, we will provide more details in the next section.

✔ **Evaluate Your Income Stability:** Gather your recent income statements and pay stubs. Consider the reliability and regularity of the sources of your income.

If your income is unpredictable, document your income history for irregular income, such as bonuses and commissions. Try compiling past earnings records with pay stubs, tax returns, or bank statements for at least the last 12 to 24 months, as lenders may need to see proof of your income.

✔ **Calculate Your Debt-to-Income Ratio (DTI):** Create a list of all your monthly repayments for your credit cards, existing loans, and other debts. Add up the total cost of these debts and then divide this amount by your gross monthly income. Multiply the result by 100, and this will give you the DTI percentage. Ideally, your DTI should be 36% or less, but some lenders will accept a higher DTI.

✔ **Assess Savings and Emergency Funds:** Gather up the statements for your savings accounts and investments to check the amounts of your total savings and emergency fund. Try setting aside at least three to six months of living expenses before committing to a loan.

✔ **Budget Analysis for Loan Affordability:** Use bank statements, receipts, and credit card statements to create a detailed monthly budget. Try to be accurate and not simply guess how much you typically spend. Add up your total expenses and deduct this amount from your monthly income after taxes. Ensure you have a comfortable amount remaining for your potential loan payment and any unforeseen expenses.

✔ **Future Financial Projections:** Consider any potential changes to your expenses or income that you may face soon. If you plan on getting married, having children, or changing jobs, you must consider the potential costs and adjust your budget to see if you can still afford a new loan.

Sample Calculation to Assess Loan Affordability

Let's practice some of the above concepts with a sample calculation. Imagine that you're considering a new personal loan with a monthly repayment of $300, and you're not anticipating any future changes to your financial situation.

Here is how you would assess your readiness:

If your monthly income is $4,000 and your existing monthly debt payments are $1,000, your DTI ratio would be 25%, which is well within the acceptable range. When you add in the new loan, your debt will rise to $1,300, but this still gives you an acceptable DTI of 32.5%

If you have savings of $10,000 and your monthly expenses and taxes add up to $2,000, then you have approximately five months of living expenses to have a sufficient buffer. Given the new loan, you can still save $700 each month.

Considering your budget, savings, and DTI, it appears that you could manage a new loan if you're okay with having only $700 remaining to save.

Credit Scores and Reports

As previously indicated, your credit score is important in qualifying for any loan. Lenders use this three-digit score to determine your creditworthiness, which shows how reliable you are at repaying debts. Scores range from 300 to 850; the better your credit history, the higher your score.

Your credit report includes your credit score and offers a more comprehensive overview of your credit history. Many banks and credit card issuers have integrated a credit score display option into their mobile apps or web applications. Check if your banks have this feature.

Factors Influencing Credit Scores

- **Payment History:** Timely payments are crucial for your credit scores. It accounts for 35% of your score. Late payments and severe issues like bankruptcy can significantly damage your score.

- **Length of Credit History:** Longer credit histories typically lead to higher credit scores. It measures the age of your oldest and newest accounts and the average age of all your accounts.

- **Credit Variety:** Having a diverse range of credit types, such as credit cards and mortgages, can positively impact your credit score. It shows your skill in effectively managing different kinds of debt.

- **Amounts Owed:** The total debt you owe and your credit utilization ratio make up 30% of your score. Lower utilization rates can help you improve your FICO score. To calculate credit utilization, we need to understand two types of credit:

  o **Revolving Credit:** Credit cards and lines of credit are the most common forms in this category. They allow you to borrow up to a limit and repay as you go, with no fixed end date.

  o **Installment Credit:** Auto loans and mortgages are the most popular forms in this group. It involves borrowing and repaying a set amount in fixed monthly payments over a set period.

Credit utilization only factors in revolving credit. Here is a sample calculation:

Suppose we have two credit cards and one personal line of credit, as shown below.

Credit card 1: Limit $6,500, Balance $1,600, Utilization 25%

Credit card 2: Limit $4,800, Balance $1,500, Utilization 31%

Personal line of credit: Limit $10,000, Balance $2,000, Utilization 20%

Total Credit Limit: $21,300

Total Balance: $5,100

Overall Utilization Rate: **23.94%**

- **New Credit:** New credit applications can slightly lower your score, as each hard inquiry may indicate potential risk, but multiple inquiries for the same type of loan within a short period are usually treated as one.

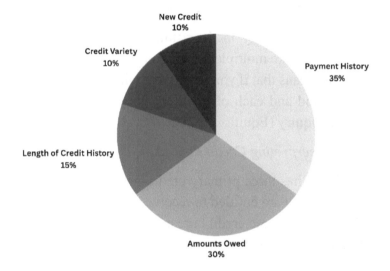

Figure 5.1 *The distribution of five categories in the FICO score (Akin, 2023).*

Types of Credit Inquiries

- **Hard Inquiry:** When a person or a financial institution, like a lender or credit card company, reviews your credit history, they usually perform a hard inquiry. Some examples are applying for a credit card, mortgage, and rental application (Devaney, 2023). Hard pulls can affect the credit score.

- **Soft Inquiry:** This inquiry commonly happens when someone or a company checks your credit as part of their background check.

Checking your credit score on credit report providers like Experian, employers conducting background checks, and pre-qualification for credit cards all fall under this category. Soft pulls do not affect your credit score. (Devaney, 2023).

Having one or two hard inquiries may cause a minor dip in your score, but it's unlikely to have a major effect. However, having multiple hard inquiries in a short period can raise a red flag (Devaney, 2023). There are usually exceptions for loans like mortgages and auto loans, as we have to shop around, and it may need multiple inquiries.

Credit scoring models vary in their time periods, but generally, it is considered safe to make multiple hard inquiries within a timeframe of 14 to 45 days. This means that if you reach out to different mortgage lenders in this short period and each of them checks your credit, they will be counted as one inquiry (Equifax, 2023).

Accessing and Interpreting Credit Reports

The United States has three primary credit bureaus: Equifax, Experian, and TransUnion. You are entitled to receive one free copy of your credit report each year from these credit bureaus. It is also possible to get your report online from sites such as annualcreditreport.com.

Once you have a copy of your report, review the following items and their accuracy (DeNicola, 2021).

- ✓ **Personal Data:** This includes your name, address, date of birth, etc.

- ✓ **Accounts:** Be sure to check for any accounts you didn't open, late payments reported incorrectly, and any other errors in your account details.

- ✓ **Inquiries:** Search for any hard inquiries that you didn't authorize.

- ✓ **Bankruptcy:** Find out if there have been any false bankruptcy filings.

Loan Application Process

Regardless of what loan you choose, the process is generally straightforward. Let's go through each step for a better understanding.

1) **Starting the Application:** Your loan journey begins by discussing your needs with a loan officer. It can be done in person or online. You'll be asked to outline your financial situation. The common practice is to complete an application. Most application forms require basic personal details, income information, and typical expenses. It can be a little more complicated if you're applying for a business loan, as you must present a market analysis and a copy of your business model.

   Most applications also require supporting documentation. This includes your ID, financial statements, tax returns, and income sources or employment details. Business loan applications may also require business plans and financial statements.

2) **Underwriting - The Review Phase:** After you submit the loan application, an underwriter will review it. The underwriter will go through your application and examine your financial background, assessing your credit history, income, and expenses. For business loans, they will also assess the financial health of your business. This evaluation is crucial to determine your eligibility for a loan.

   After the underwriter has gone through your application, they will issue an approval decision. Hopefully, you'll be approved and move on to the next step.

3) **Closing the Loan:** You will move on to the loan closure stage after approval. All the required legal documents, including the loan agreement, have been prepared at this stage. They will give you a list of necessary documents to finalize your loan. If you don't submit the documents on time, it will delay the final closing and the speed at which you receive the funds.

Interest Rates and APR

When considering any type of loan, you'll frequently encounter two terms: interest rate and APR (annual percentage rate). It can feel confusing, as it's easy to assume that interest rate and APR are the same. However, knowing their differences can help you better understand the true cost of borrowing.

The **interest rate** is a percentage of the total loan or principal amount. It is the amount a lender charges the borrower for using their money over a specified period.

The **APR** represents a bigger picture of the costs of your loan. It includes the interest rate and any other expenses relating to the loan, such as origination fees, closing costs, or mortgage points (Interest Rate and the APR, 2024).

Generally, APR will be higher than the interest rate as it provides a clearer picture of the yearly cost of the loan. However, in some cases, when there are no additional fees or closing costs, the interest rate and APR can be the same.

Lenders calculate your interest rate based on factors such as your credit score, loan type, DTI, etc. To calculate the APR, lenders add up the interest rate along with any other loan-related fees. For example, an auto loan with a 7.5% interest rate may have an APR of 7.8% once the additional fees are factored in.

While your personal financial circumstances do impact your rates, both interest rates and APRs are subject to broader economic trends. When rates are high in the marketplace, you'll be offered a higher rate compared to times when rates are lower, even if your circumstances are exactly the same. It's a good idea to compare numbers from different lenders to find the best deal for you, as their criteria can vary.

Loan Fees and Costs

Unfortunately (but not surprisingly), there are more costs involved in getting a loan than simply repaying the amount you borrow. Make sure you know the different costs and fees that could apply to you.

Common Loan Fees and Costs

- **Origination Fees:** The lenders charge this fee to process your loan application. It usually covers the cost of credit checks and other application expenses.

- **Application Fees:** Certain lenders charge a fee simply for reviewing your application. In this case, you may incur a fee regardless of whether your application is approved.

- **Closing Costs:** This usually only applies to mortgages, home loans, and home equity loans. Closing costs cover the fees for title searches, property appraisals, and other expenses.

- **Late Payment Fees:** Most lenders impose a fee if you skip a payment or don't pay according to your loan schedule. The fee can vary a lot and might increase if you're late more than once.

- **Prepayment Fees:** Some lenders charge a fee if you pay off your loan early. It can include making overpayments or clearing the account entirely. This fee compensates the lender for interest they won't collect on your account.

If you want to reduce these fees, it's a good idea to compare options and talk to several lenders. Moreover, don't hesitate to negotiate the fees with them, especially if you already have a favorable offer from one lender. You can leverage that offer to negotiate with other lenders and possibly have your expenses waived or reduced. The same principle also applies to interest rates. Request quotes from multiple lenders and see if they can beat the competitors. By negotiating, you can potentially save thousands of dollars overtime.

Final Thoughts

Love them or hate them, loans are a reality in our financial world. From personal loans to mortgages, we may deal with them in some shape or form. However, by being proactive and getting to know them, we can avoid making poor decisions and enduring financial losses. In the next chapter, we'll discuss a more common form of borrowing: credit cards.

Chapter 6

Mastering Credit Cards

———•———————•———

"As a child, a library card takes you to exotic, faraway places. When you're grown up, a credit card does it." ~ *Sam Ewing*

It is widely agreed that credit cards offer one of the most convenient payment methods. From paying bills to buying things online, many of us use credit cards to handle these financial obligations. Despite the convenience, how many young people do you think are fully knowledgeable about all aspects of their credit cards? Unfortunately, many are not. A recent study from LendEDU reported that less than 10 percent of the college students who participated knew the interest rate on their credit cards. (Jaracz, n.d.)

This chapter will delve into lesser-known or overlooked information about credit cards.

Credit Cards vs. Debit Cards: Card Safety

Credit and debit cards may appear alike; after all, they have a similar 16-digit number, expiration date, and name printed across the front. However, their functions are quite different. While you likely have a solid understanding of the differences between credit cards and debit cards in terms of where the money comes from, you may not be aware of the differences regarding safety and liability.

Some people may feel more comfortable using a debit card. However, credit cards actually have the upper hand in terms of liability. The Fair Credit Billing Act (FCBA) has a liability cap for unauthorized charges of $50, and some credit card issuers take this a step further and provide zero liability for fraudulent charges.

Debit cards have a different form of protection. The Electronic Fund Transfer Act (EFTA) does offer fraud protection, but there is a catch: you need to act quickly. If you report your card lost or stolen within two days, the liability is capped at $50, but if you delay, the liability cap could reach $500 or more.

Fraudulent transactions with your debit card can have an immediate impact on your bank balance. If you have an unauthorized charge on your debit card, checks could bounce, and payments could be declined, which can lead to bank charges. It can be difficult to get your money back, at least not immediately or at all.

On the flip side, credit cards provide greater flexibility. Typically, disputed charges are promptly credited back after an investigation, restoring your available credit limit.

Understanding Credit Card Interest and APR

Knowing the interest, APR, and repayment terms of various credit cards can help you select the ideal card and prevent unexpected fees and charges.

When you look at your credit card account details, the first thing you'll likely see is the APR or Annual Percentage Rate. This number tells you exactly how much it will cost to borrow money on a credit card for one year. The APR includes not only the basic interest rate but also any other charges or fees that may apply. This provides a complete picture of what you will pay.

Credit cards tend to have different types of APRs: one for purchases, one for any cash advances, and even possibly one for balance transfers. Some cards also offer introductory rates. These are like welcome deals for signing up for a new card. You may get a low or 0% APR for a limited time, but remember that after this introductory period, the regular APR will kick in.

How APRs are Calculated

Credit card companies typically waive interest charges on purchases if you consistently pay your full balance by the due date. However, if you have an outstanding balance, interest will usually start accumulating on purchases immediately and will be included at the end of each billing period (Habits, 2023).

Here is what the calculation may look like. Let's assume your credit card has a 19% APR for purchases, and you have an average $3,000 daily balance.

First, we need to calculate the daily rate.

$$\text{Daily Rate} = 19\% \div 365 = 0.052\%$$

Credit cards have different billing cycles, varying from 28 to 31 days (DeNicola, 2022). Let's say your card has 28-day billing cycles. Now, we can calculate the total interest for this credit card.

$$\text{Total Interest} = 0.052\% \times \$3,000 \times 28 = \$43.68$$

Remember, APR doesn't consider the effects of compounding. Compounding occurs when interest is added to your overall owed balance, meaning you must pay interest for the bigger balance.

Every credit card and credit card issuer has their own fees that factor into their APR calculations. It's essential that you read the terms and conditions to fully understand what's included and avoid any 'surprise' fees when it's time to pay your bill.

The Ultimate Costs of Minimum Payments

When you hold a credit card, your statement shows the total amount you owe and the minimum payment amount. The minimum payment isn't a random number; your credit card issuer uses a formula to calculate it. The minimum payment is the least amount you need to pay to stay in good standing with the creditor. When getting a new credit card, it would be helpful to understand how they calculate the minimum payment.

Some companies use a flat percentage, while others add in interest and fees accrued on your last statement. The most common method is a percentage of the balance plus fees and interest added to the account during the billing period.

Here's an example:

Your credit card has a balance of $2,000, and the issuer calculates the minimum payment as 1% of the balance plus fees and interest.

Let's assume for this example that your APR is 18%, and there are no other fees. This means your minimum payment would be $50 (1% of $2,000 is $20, and the $30 is for interest).

Although you are only required to make the minimum payment on your credit card accounts each month, solely doing this can significantly affect your debt.

In the previous example, that $2,000 credit card balance would only reduce to $1980, even though you paid $50. It is because you only paid off 1% of the balance, and the rest covered the interest. So, if you continued only to pay the minimum after six months, you would still have a credit card balance of approximately $1,882.96 despite paying $292.60 to your credit card company (see Table 6.1).

Month	Initial Balance	Interest	Principal Payment	Minimum Payment	New Balance
1	$2,000.00	$30.00	$20.00	$50.00	$1,980.00
2	$1,980.00	$29.70	$19.80	$49.50	$1,960.20
3	$1,960.20	$29.40	$19.60	$49.00	$1,940.60
4	$1,940.60	$29.11	$19.41	$48.52	$1,921.19
5	$1,921.19	$28.82	$19.21	$48.03	$1,901.98
6	$1,901.98	$28.53	$19.02	$47.55	$1,882.96
Total		$175.56	$117.04	$292.60	

Table 6.1 The breakdown of 6-month credit card payments.

If you want to get out of this cycle, pay more than the minimum amount due whenever possible. Even paying a little extra can significantly impact reducing your overall debt and the interest you'll pay. If you are having trouble paying more than the minimum, look at your budget to see if there are areas where you can cut back to pay down your credit card balance faster.

Understanding Credit Card Billing Cycles

Now, let's examine your credit card statement and how to understand billing cycles. Your statement includes more than just a simple list of card transactions. The following are what to look for in your statement. While the names may differ, most credit cards have these sections.

- **Account Activity Summary:** This is a financial snapshot showing the details of your account status. It includes purchases, payments, balance transfers, and more. You can use the account activity summary to check your new balance, the available credit, and the closing date of your billing cycle.

- **Payment Information:** This section details the total new balance and your minimum payment requirement. Review your credit card terms, but payments received by 5:00 p.m. on the due date are usually on time. If the due date falls on a weekend or a holiday, making a payment by 5:00 p.m. the following business day will be on time.

- **Late Payment Warnings:** This section details the implications of making late payments. You'll find information about additional fees or higher interest rates that will apply if your payment is late.

- **Interests Charged:** This part shows how much interest has been calculated on your balance. If there are different APRs for different balance types, such as standard purchases and cash advances, then they will appear separately.

- **Interest Rate Change Notification:** If you have triggered a penalty rate or the credit card issuer changes your interest rate, you'll see a notification with 45 days of notice. You may also see notifications for any other adjustments to your account terms. As with interest rate changes, your card issuer must provide a minimum of 45 days of notice (The Federal Reserve Board, 2010).

Grace and Interest-Free Periods

Another important aspect of understanding your credit card statement is the grace or interest-free periods. A grace period on your credit card is like hitting a financial pause button, as it provides a valuable window that is interest-free. This period typically runs from the end of your billing cycle until the payment due date. If you paid the bill in the previous month on time and in full, you would enjoy this interest-free period.

Let's put this into context with an example. If your billing cycle ends on May 31st and the payment is due on June 22nd, your grace period spans these two dates. If you pay your full card balance by June 22nd, you won't accrue interest on the money you borrowed during this billing cycle.

If you *don't* pay the full balance, the grace period does not go into effect anymore, and you'll incur interest charges on the unpaid balance and any new purchases. Moreover, grace periods typically don't cover balance transfers or cash advances, which often begin immediately accruing interest (Kagan, 2019, Grace Period).

Avoiding Late Fees and Managing Due Dates

If you have multiple credit cards, managing the due dates for the various cards can be a bit of a juggling act. To avoid getting into a mess, create a master list of all your cards with their due dates.

The 2009 Card Act ensures that payments for an individual credit card fall on the same date each month to bring consistency to your financial routine, and you could request a change in the due date for one or more cards to align better with your salary payment or distribute payments more evenly throughout the month.

Another good strategy is to set up auto payment for your account. This essentially delegates the responsibility of making payments on time to your bank. You can pay the full balance or opt for the minimum payment to prevent charges.

If you prefer a manual approach, create payment reminders. You can sign up for the reminder services offered by your credit card company to receive email or SMS messages reminding you of current, upcoming, or even past-due payment dates. Remember, making payments on time is important for maintaining a good credit score.

What If You Miss a Credit Card Payment?

Despite the best efforts, sometimes a payment can fall through the cracks. If you miss a payment, don't panic and take decisive action.

- **Make a Payment ASAP:** Once you realize you've missed a

payment, try to make a payment as soon as possible. Although there may be a fee for a payment that is a day or two late, it will not immediately affect your credit score. Typically, a late payment will only be reported to the credit bureaus when it reaches 30 days past due (DeNicola, 2019). By paying as quickly as possible, you can avoid significant credit issues.

- **Speak to Your Card Company:** If you have a good track record of making your payments on time, contact your credit card company. In this situation, your card issuer may waive a late fee. They can also explain if you've triggered any penalty interest rates and how to revert to the regular rate.

- **Monitor Your Credit Report:** A late payment can be a stain on your credit report for as long as seven years. Check your credit report regularly to understand the impact of late payments and develop strategies for your future financial health.

How to Choose the Right Credit Card

If there's one thing we can all agree on, it's that there is an overwhelming amount of credit cards on the market, and finding the perfect option can seem nearly impossible. You certainly don't want to make a false start with something so important! The key is to get a credit card that matches your spending habits and financial needs.

Consider these factors when applying for your first or next credit card:

- **Your Credit Score:** Perhaps one of the most important elements in choosing the right credit card is your credit score. It will determine your eligibility for certain cards. If you have a higher score, you can access the cards which offer better benefits. Those with a lower credit score may have fewer options, but if you focus on applying for the right cards, you won't have multiple inquiries on your credit report.

- **Your Needs:** There are generally three main types of cards: ones that save on interest, those that improve limited or damaged credit, and those that earn rewards. You should choose a card that meets your needs and is most appropriate to your lifestyle. For example, if you rarely travel, a travel card will not be of much use. There are comparison tools on credit card websites and platforms like NerdWallet that can filter the options according to your credit score and preferences.

- **Compare the Details:** Once you've narrowed down your options, it's time to compare the card details. In general, first, look at interest rates, fees, and charges for all credit card types. Then, depending on your goal, you may also consider the following details.

  o If you're applying for a low or 0% interest card, check the length of the zero or low introductory APR period. The longer the period, the more you can save on interest. Confirm that the ongoing interest rate is reasonable once the introductory period is over.

  o If you aim to build credit, determine whether it's a secured or unsecured card. Secured cards require a deposit, which becomes your credit limit. Also, verify if you can switch to an unsecured card after showing responsible usage.

  o For reward cards, evaluate how to earn rewards and the earning rate. Also, ensure you know how to redeem them and if there are any limitations or expiration dates.

Understanding Credit Card Rewards and Offers

One of the main reasons people are interested in getting a new credit card is to access the rewards program or welcome offers. Some very lucrative rewards programs are on the market, and choosing the right card and program can benefit you.

Cashback

Cashback is one of the simplest forms of credit card rewards. Depending on the reward tiers, you can receive a certain percentage or dollar amount of money back on your spending. This means that you may earn 6% back on spending in categories like travel or groceries and 1% on other spending.

There are also other types of cashback cards that reward you twice. You'll earn a cashback amount when you make a purchase and another cashback amount when you pay off your purchases.

Reward Miles

Many credit cards have a partnership agreement with particular airlines or travel brands. It's similar to cashback, but instead of cash, you earn rewards to purchase plane tickets. Some cards offer bonus points if you meet a spending requirement or other conditions as a welcome offer. So, it is worth checking the terms and conditions to make sure you don't miss out.

Intro Rate Cards

These cards are generally best for those transferring a balance from another card or interested in making a large purchase. Essentially, you'll be paying a low or 0% APR for a specific period. For example, you may not pay interest for up to 12 months. You must look out for the small print on these cards, though. Some only offer the introductory rate for balance transfers, which need to be made within a certain time of opening the card account. Also, watch out for a balance transfer fee.

Benefits Package

In addition to the credit card rewards, your new card may also offer a benefits package. This can vary significantly from card to card but could include features like rental car insurance, flight upgrades, free subscriptions, and more. Of course, you should check that these benefits are useful for you, as there is no point in choosing a card with a higher annual fee or a higher APR if you won't get the most value from the card perks.

How Credit Cards Impact Credit Scores

Credit cards are more than a simple, convenient payment method; they play a significant role in shaping your credit. You need to understand how using credit cards can impact your credit score so you can keep tabs on your overall short- and long-term financial health.

Late Payments

We've already covered this, but it is important to reiterate that late or missed payments are recorded on your credit report. Plus, a history of making timely payments can show potential lenders that you can handle your credit responsibly.

Credit Utilization

Try to keep your credit card utilization ratio below 30%. This means that if your card has a $15,000 limit, you should have a balance of $5,000 or less.

Getting a new credit card and paying the bill in full each month can reduce the overall utilization percentage (Morris, 2021). High credit utilization and maxing out credit accounts can raise red flags for lenders, so it's best to avoid them.

Final Thoughts

Now that we've covered the ins and outs of finding and managing credit cards, it's time to think bigger. We briefly discussed mortgages in the previous chapter, but Chapter 7 is dedicated to this topic.

Chapter 7

Getting Mortgage-Ready

———————•———————

"If I knew where I was going to want to live the next five or ten years, I would buy a home, and I'd finance it with a 30-year mortgage. It's a terrific deal." ~ Warren Buffett

Mortgages can be intimidating to young individuals, but learning how they function is essential for owning a home. Getting a head start on understanding them can decrease stress during the decision-making process. In this chapter, we'll explore how to get yourself mortgage-ready for this next step in your financial journey.

Mortgage Basics

Buying a home is likely to be your largest investment in your lifetime, so you'll need a specialized loan to help you with the purchase. A mortgage allows you to repay the funds needed to buy the home with regular payments split into principal and interest, using the property as collateral for the loan. That makes it a secured loan, which we covered in Chapter 5.

Since mortgages are typically for very large amounts, applicants need to meet some understandably rigid criteria, including good credit scores, ability to make a down payment, and income requirements. There is also a detailed underwriting and evaluation process.

There are various companies and services that can help you get your mortgage. Here are the most prominent ones:

- **Conventional banks:** They are the traditional choice for a mortgage. If you are already a customer, a mortgage from your existing bank can feel simpler and easier to manage.

- **Credit Unions:** Credit Unions are like banks but have members rather than customers. Members have a stake in the credit union, so they are also partial owners. For this reason, a credit union can offer exclusive benefits, including mortgage deals.

- **Mortgage Brokers:** If you want help comparing mortgage deals from various lenders, a mortgage broker could appeal to you. Brokers can advise you on the available loan options from across the marketplace and assist you with managing the documents, but they usually come with additional fees. Your realtor or a financial advisor can put you in touch with a mortgage broker in your area.

- **Non-Bank Mortgage Lenders:** These lenders are generally online and offer fast and flexible loan options, including mortgages. Non-bank mortgage lenders have exclusive relationships with mortgage providers throughout the market. This can be especially appealing if you need a nonconventional loan or have complex credit needs.

- **Mortgage Marketplaces:** These platforms enable you to compare different lenders' offers and interest rates. You can often find these platforms online (e.g., Bankrate, Nerdwallet). It can be a convenient way to shop for the best mortgage terms.

Choosing the right provider for your mortgage depends on your preferences and circumstances. Whether you prefer the familiarity of dealing with your local bank, the personalized service of a credit union, or the convenience of an online lender, the choice is yours.

The Mortgage Process

It can feel nerve-wracking to start the mortgage process, but once you have the keys to a new home, it will all feel worth it. Although every lender's specific details will vary, the basic steps of getting a mortgage look like this:

Pre-Approval

Before you start the application process, you must evaluate the different types of mortgages and decide which one is best for you. Online tools like mortgage calculators can help you estimate monthly repayments based on the type of mortgage, the interest rate, the down payment, and the home price. Once you have an idea of what you are looking for, you can approach lenders for pre-approval. This will give you a clear picture of what you can afford, and pre-approval will show sellers that you are a serious buyer.

Find Your New Home

Once you have pre-approval, you can start shopping for your dream home. You can speak to a realtor, use online platforms, or even explore auctions or off-market opportunities. Attend an open house or a showing to see the property for yourself. If you find a home you can picture yourself living in, it is time to make an offer. Your offer should be within your budget but don't forget you'll need to plan for some contingencies. You may need to pay for the home inspection, appraisals, and other unexpected expenses.

Mortgage Application

If your offer is accepted, it is time to apply for your mortgage officially. The mortgage application is a detailed document that you submit to the lender. It includes information about your financial status, employment history, and property. This information provides the lender with a comprehensive snapshot of your readiness for a mortgage.

Before you begin the application, it is essential to gather all your financial information and paperwork; having everything in one place makes the process that much less stressful. Most U.S. lenders use the Uniform Residential Loan Application or 1003 Mortgage Application. You can find examples of this form online to see the type of detail you'll need to provide.

The primary sections of this form include:

- **Borrower Information:** This includes your full name, address, marital status, dependents, etc.

- **Financial Details:** This covers assets and debts, including bank accounts, credit cards, loans, and if you own any other assets, such as real estate.

- **Property Details:** You need to provide the property address, the loan type, and rental income details if you're buying this property as an investment.

- **Declarations:** This section discloses any financial or legal matters not previously covered in the application and clarifies your intentions for the property.

- **Agreement:** Finally, you need to sign off on the application confirming that all the details you've provided are truthful and accurate.

Remember that your credit will be checked, so be sure your credit report is in the best possible shape. After you submit your application, you will receive a standardized loan estimate. (Graham, n.d.).

Confirm if the lender will do a "Hard" credit check (see chapter 5). This inquiry appears on your credit report. Therefore, to minimize the impact on your credit score, shop multiple lenders within a short period (Cfp & Metzger, 2024).

The Underwriting Process

Once you've submitted your paperwork, the application and supporting documentation will be sent to the underwriting team. The underwriter is the key decision-maker. They will assess your application in detail and require an appraisal of the property to ensure the application and mortgage deal are viable.

Closing

This is the exciting final step in the process, as you are now *close to home ownership.* You'll need to carefully review the closing disclosure form to ensure you have accounted for all the costs. Closing costs are typically 2% to 6% of the loan amount (Marquand, 2024). If everything is in order, you sign the paperwork, and soon, you'll be handed the keys to your new home!

It is worth mentioning that the financial industry has regulations in place to ensure non-discrimination. It means that mortgage lender discrimination is both unethical and illegal. If you suspect you faced discrimination based on your personal characteristics, you can report it to the CFPB (Consumer Financial Protection Bureau) (Consumer Financial Protection Bureau, 2023).

Exploring the Different Types of Mortgages

When assessing mortgages, three key elements are loan type, interest rate type, and loan duration (Different Kinds of Loans, n.d.).

Loan Types

- **Conventional:** This is the most common type. Most private lenders offer these mortgages, and borrowers can use them for various types of properties. They typically require a good credit score.

- **Jumbo:** To finance a property with a price surpassing your state's Federal Housing Finance Agency's (FHFA) annual limit, you must apply for a Jumbo loan (Dehan, 2024). For instance, if you are seeking an $800,000 loan, but the FHFA has set the maximum limit in your area at $700,000, you must apply for a jumbo loan.

- **Government-Backed:** Several types of government-backed

mortgage loans provide a more flexible option for applicants.

- o *FHA Loans:* A good option if you have a lower credit score and less available cash to use as a down payment. However, you will need to pay mortgage insurance premiums (Marquand, 2024)

- o *VA Loans:* Exclusive to members and veterans of the U.S. military, these benefits include perks like waived mortgage insurance and no obligation for a minimum down payment (Department of Veterans Affairs, n.d.)

- o *USDA Loans:* Designed for individuals with moderate to low incomes, specifically those living in rural areas. These loans do not have any minimum down payment requirements (Green, 2024).

Interest Rate Types

- **Fixed Rates:** Most borrowers select fixed-rate mortgages as their top choice. If you prefer a reliable and predictable monthly payment structure for your loan, especially in the long term, a fixed-rate loan would be the recommended option. With a fixed-rate loan, you won't have to worry about fluctuations in your monthly principal and interest payments as they stay consistent. It's important to note that your monthly costs can still change due to factors such as increases or decreases in property taxes, homeowner's insurance, mortgage insurance, etc. (Different Kinds of Loans, n.d.).

- **ARMs (Adjustable-Rate Mortgages):** These mortgages offer a fixed introductory rate, which is initially low but then adjusted at predetermined intervals. The 5/1 ARM loan is one example of an adjustable-rate mortgage.

During the first five years, the 5/1 ARM has a fixed interest rate, and afterward, it adjusts once per year until the loan is fully paid off.

If you only intend to own your home for a few years or expect an increase in your future earnings, this specific mortgage can be a viable option. Moreover, if the interest rate for a fixed-rate mortgage is unreasonably high, it might be beneficial to consider this alternative (FHA Adjustable Rate Mortgage - HUD, n.d.).

Loan Duration

While the interest rate gets a lot of attention, the duration of the mortgage is equally, if not more, important. Different choices are available in the market, but the two most common mortgage durations in the United States are 15 and 30 years. The following are the general pros and cons for each option:

15-Year Mortgage: Pros and Cons

Pros:

- **Less Interest Paid Overall:** Because of the shorter timeline, you will pay significantly less interest than longer-term loans.

- **Build Equity Quickly:** Since it's a shorter loan, you'll be paying more principal each month, which means your property's equity will increase faster.

- **Lower Interest Rates:** Lenders typically offer lower interest rates on 15-year mortgages because it is less risky for them.

Cons:

- **Higher Monthly Payments:** Choosing a shorter term means you'll have to make higher monthly payments. It can put a lot of pressure on your budget, so keep that in mind, especially if your income isn't stable or you have other important expenses.

- **Limits Your Financial Goals:** High monthly payments leave less room for other financial goals, like saving for retirement, investing, or managing unforeseen expenses.

30-Year Mortgage: Pros and Cons

Pros:

- **Lower Monthly Payments:** By extending the loan term to 30 years, monthly payments are reduced, making homeownership more achievable.

- **Flexibility:** You can always choose to make extra payments toward the principal to pay off your loan earlier without committing to a higher monthly obligation. Furthermore, you can use the extra cash toward your savings or investment goals.

- **Tax Deductible Interest:** This deduction is more significant in the early years of a 30-year loan than the other option, as your interest payment would be higher.

Cons:

- **More Interest Paid Over Time:** Choosing a longer term will cause higher interest payments throughout the loan's duration.

- **Slower Equity Building:** It takes longer to build equity in your home due to paying more interest in the beginning. This might work against you if you intend to sell your home within a few years or if the value of homes in the area drops after you make the purchase.

Important Mortgage Terms

Exploring new topics always involves learning new terms. Mortgages are no different and come with their own set of terms and phrases. Here are some common terms you'll often encounter when looking for a mortgage.

- **Amortization:** This complex term simply refers to the process of paying off your mortgage according to your regular payment schedule. Most of the time, you'll decrease the outstanding mortgage amount with each payment.

- In Table 7.1, we can see the amortization schedule of a $300,000 loan with 5% interest. The table shows only the first, middle, and last four months of the payment schedule.

When looking at the interest column, it is apparent that at the start of repayment, our payments are mainly directed towards interest and gradually shift towards the principal. This is particularly important to note when you decide to refinance the loan as this schedule resets, and you start paying more interest again.

Date	Principal	Interest	Remaining Balance
Feb-2023	$360.46	$1,250.00	$299,639.54
Mar-2023	$361.97	$1,248.50	$299,277.57
Apr-2023	$363.48	$1,246.99	$298,914.09
May-2023	$364.99	$1,245.48	$298,549.10
Feb-2038	$761.92	$848.55	$202,889.81
Mar-2038	$765.09	$845.37	$202,124.72
Apr-2038	$768.28	$842.19	$201,356.44
May-2038	$771.48	$838.99	$200,584.96
Oct-2052	$1,583.90	$26.56	$4,791.41
Nov-2052	$1,590.50	$19.96	$3,200.91
Dec-2052	$1,597.13	$13.34	$1,603.78
Jan-2053	$1,603.78	$6.68	$0.00

Table 7.1 *Example of an Amortization Schedule*

- **Closing Disclosure:** This is a crucial document that details the final terms of the mortgage, including the length of the loan, the monthly payments, and the amount of the closing costs (Bell, 2024). You should compare this document to each loan deal to evaluate which one is best for you.

- **Loan-to-Value Ratio:** The LTV is the amount of the mortgage compared to the appraised value of the property. Lenders use the LTV to determine loan approval and if mortgage insurance is needed. If you have a higher down payment, you will automatically lower the LTV. For example, if your home has an appraised value of $200,000 and you've put $20,000 down, your mortgage is $180,000, and your LTV is 90%. However, putting $50,000 down is 25% of the appraised value, bringing your LTV down to 75%.

While understanding mortgage terms can help, you don't need to become an expert overnight, and you can ask your lender for clarification if you're unsure.

Understanding Down Payments and Mortgage Insurance

When buying a home, you cannot underestimate the significance of a down payment. The amount of money you put down will affect your mortgage in the long run. Your down payment is the stake you put into your new home and signifies your commitment to potential lenders.

Putting down a larger down payment reduces the risk for the lender since you have more to lose if you default on the loan. With this lower risk, the lender often offers lower interest rates, and you can enjoy lower payments.

The minimum down payment will vary based on the type of mortgage or home loan you opt for.

- **Conventional Loans:** This can vary according to the lender, but the minimum can be as low as 3% (Buczynski & Wood, 2024).

- **FHA Loans:** These have a minimum of 3.5%, but you need a credit score of at least 580 (FHA Loan, n.d.).

- **USDA and VA Loans:** These loans can have a zero down payment requirement (Nmls, 2024).

Since having a larger down payment offers some great benefits, it's a good idea to aim for putting down more than the minimum requirement. The optimal down payment will depend on your comfort level and financial situation.

While a higher down payment can give you access to certain advantages, it's important to avoid exhausting your savings. You may need extra cash to cover your closing costs and any unexpected expenses associated with home ownership. So consider your complete financial situation to assess how much you can comfortably afford.

It's important to note that using your emergency funds as a down payment is not a smart choice. Their sole purpose is to protect you in case of an emergency.

Mortgage Insurance

Another important aspect of finding the optimum down payment amount is mortgage insurance. Mortgage insurance is a financial safety net designed to protect the lender if you cannot meet the mortgage obligations. Since your lender is taking on the bulk of the financial burden for your new home, they need a shield against unforeseen events, such as defaulting on your payments.

There are several types of mortgage insurance:

- **PMI (Private Mortgage Insurance):** If your down payment for a conventional mortgage is less than 20%, you will probably have to get PMI. Lenders will automatically remove it when your LTV drops below 78%. However, you can request them to remove it when you hit the 80% LTV (Ostrowski, 2024).

  Typically, lenders calculate the loan-to-value ratio based on the house's original value. However, if you have made renovations that have increased the value of your property or if the market has experienced growth, you can request a reassessment to check if your LTV ratio has decreased (Luthi, 2023).

Your lender may have additional restrictions, so confirm with them.

- **MIP (Mortgage Insurance Premium):** MIP is mandatory if you are looking at FHA mortgages. By putting in a 10% down payment, you will pay MIP for the first 11 years. For down payments of less than 10%, the MIP will extend to the entire loan term or 30 years, whichever comes first (Dollarhide, 2024).

- **Mortgage Protection Life Insurance:** Insurance companies typically offer this insurance as an add-on option after completing the home purchase. The insurance will cover the remaining balance if you pass away before fully paying your mortgage (Martin, 2024).

Credit Score Considerations

As with all lending products, your credit score is crucial, but it has even greater significance for a mortgage. While lenders have their own minimum credit score requirements, most people who qualify have a score in the 650-plus range. The higher your score, the more loan options you'll have.

The minimum credit score requirements can be influenced by the type of loan you're applying for (Crace, 2024).

- **Conventional Loans:** Generally, you will need a credit score of at least 620, but the higher your score, the more likely you get lower interest rates.

- **FHA Loans:** These tend to be more lenient. You may qualify with a score in the 500s, but scores of 580 or more can have more options.

- **USDA and VA Loans:** While there are no specific credit score requirements, a score above 640 is typically needed for USDA loans and 580 or higher for VA loans.

Locking in a Mortgage Interest Rate

The interest rate significantly affects mortgage payments and total loan costs. Locking in your interest rate can be helpful because it assures you that your rate won't change between receiving your offer and closing time. If your application remains unchanged and you close within the specified time frame, you'll have peace of mind regarding potential rate increases.

The lock-in process involves the following steps (Araj, n.d.).

- **Get Mortgage Approval:** As mentioned in the mortgage application section, ensure you provide your lender with all the necessary documents.

- **Lock-in Request:** When you get the approval, you can request a rate lock from the lender. Your lender will confirm the lock-in period and your rate. Lock periods typically last 30 to 60 days.

Considerations for Rate Locks

While a rate lock may seem like a simple decision, there are a few things to consider. First, some lenders impose a charge for locking in a rate, especially if it's over a longer period. Will the fee offset or overtake your savings from a rate lock? It's essential to assess what is most cost-effective for you. You should also consider when to lock in your rate, especially if you are close to buying a home and the rates are favorable. If you lock in too early, you could risk the lock expiring before closing. Finally, if you think rates may drop, you could choose to float your rate, but this carries the risk of rates increasing.

Remember that you still have flexibility and can switch lenders even after locking in a rate. If you find better terms, you can switch to another lender. Some lenders will also offer "float down" options if rates drop, but you may incur additional fees. Mortgage rate locks can provide a valuable tool, offering stability in a fluctuating market so you can plan your finances more accurately. Nevertheless, it is crucial to factor in the potential costs and timing to maximize its benefits.

Understanding Mortgage Escrow

Some lenders might ask you to have an escrow account with your mortgage. As you know, besides the mortgage payment, you must also pay for home insurance, property taxes, and mortgage insurance, if applicable.

To guarantee timely payment, lenders may estimate the monthly amount and add it to your mortgage payment. They save this extra money into an account called escrow.

Lenders often require an additional cushion of funds in the escrow account. It is typically the equivalent of two months of payments to cover any unexpected cost increases. State and federal laws regulate the cushion amount.

Every year, they go through your account, and if there's extra money, you might get it back or use it for future payments. On the other hand, if there is a shortfall, you'll receive a bill for the difference.

Not every mortgage requires an escrow account. Lenders typically use LTVs to determine if an account is necessary. If the amount you owe on your mortgage is less than 80% of the value of your home, you might have the option to handle insurance and tax payments yourself. This means you must save money to pay these expenses on time. Failure to pay can have serious consequences, including loss of coverage, penalties, or tax liens.

While an escrow account can be convenient, you may prefer to put this amount into a high-yield savings account each month. Doing so means you'll have the money to cover the bills each year, and until they are due, you'll earn some interest.

Strategies to Pay Off a Mortgage Faster

A mortgage represents a significant debt. While they typically have a lower rate compared to other types of loans, with such long terms, you can accumulate substantial interest on the account. Therefore, developing strategies to pay off your mortgage faster for long-term financial freedom is a good idea.

- **Refinance:** If rates have dropped or your credit score has significantly improved, it could be beneficial to refinance at a lower rate. This will allow you to keep your monthly payments at approximately the same amount, but you'll have a shorter loan term. For example, let's say your current mortgage is $1500 per month. The interest rate significantly goes down, and if you refinance, the payment will be $1300. If you keep paying $1500 each month, the additional $200 will reduce the principal and shorten the loan's life. Remember to consider the caveat regarding the refinance discussed in the Amortization section.

- **Make Extra Payments:** Extra payments, particularly early on, can have a massive impact on your loan principal. You can make a lump sum payment or work out how to make 13 payments a year rather than 12. This is a budget-friendly method, as you divide your monthly payment by 12 and add this to your regular monthly payment. You'll have made an extra payment at the end of the year, potentially shaving years off your mortgage term.

- **Round-Up:** Another simple and effective way to pay off your mortgage faster is to round up your payments to the nearest hundred.

- **Use Unexpected Income:** If you receive unexpected money, such as a tax refund or bonus, pay it into your mortgage account. It will help you pay down the mortgage principal without affecting your monthly budget.

By paying off your mortgage early, you will pay less interest over time and obtain a stronger position to manage other aspects of your finances. However, when considering this strategy, it is crucial to consider your other financial obligations.

Suppose you have a substantial amount of debt with high interest rates, such as credit cards or an auto loan. In that case, it is advisable to prioritize paying off those debts before focusing on your low-interest, long-term mortgage debt. In addition, before making any extra payments, it is important to have your emergency fund in place and ensure that you successfully achieve your other savings goals.

Opportunity Cost

People often overlook the concept of opportunity cost, which refers to the benefits lost when one option is selected over another. It applies to businesses, individuals, and investors (Fernando, 2024).

You can calculate the opportunity cost by subtracting the highest expected return of an investment from the alternative options. For example, say you have two options for investing. The expected return for the first option is $10,000, while the second choice is estimated at $5,000 for the same investment. If you choose the second option, the opportunity cost would be $5,000. In other words, your poor investment decision resulted in a loss of $5,000.

Likewise, before making extra mortgage payments or paying it off entirely, it's worth exploring alternative investment options with potentially higher returns.

Of course, we cannot predict opportunity costs with certainty, but considering them can lead to better decision-making. Just like with any other financial decision, if you're unsure, it's recommended to seek the advice of a professional.

Mortgage Question Cheat Sheet

We covered a lot in this chapter. To simplify your future references, here's a list of questions you may ask the lenders to help you find the ideal mortgage.

1. Which mortgage option would be the most suitable for my needs?

2. What are my options for the down payment?

3. I would like to know the details of my interest rate and APR.

4. Is there going to be a hard credit check?

5. Is it required to have mortgage insurance?

6. What is the breakdown of my monthly payment?

7. Do I need to have a mortgage escrow account?

8. Can you share the costs for which I will be responsible?

9. Can I lock in the rate? In that case, when does it expire?

10. What is the estimated closing date for the loan?

Final Thoughts

Mortgages can feel a little scary because they're a big financial commitment. This is particularly true if you're just starting. However, buying a home is not your only option. In the next chapter, we'll help you compare homeownership and renting to help you decide which is best for you.

Chapter 8

Buying vs. Rent

———————•———————

"Owning a home is a keystone of wealth—both financial affluence and emotional security." ~ Suze Orman

Having your own place is crucial for your independence, but it also influences your finances. Deciding between renting or buying can affect your financial situation in the long run, so a thorough comparison is necessary to make the best choice. In this chapter, we'll compare mortgages and rent, helping you gather all the information you need to choose the right housing option.

The Advantages of Renting

Renting a home is often the first choice for young adults entering the real world, and it's a smart move because of its various advantages.

Generally, renting is a less stressful option. You can avoid the burdens of homeownership, like property taxes, maintenance expenses, and home insurance. Additionally, it can decrease your responsibilities and give you some financial relief.

The property manager or owner will take care of any issues you face as a tenant, whether it's a plumbing problem or a broken appliance, and they will cover most of the expenses. As a renter, you will have no financial responsibilities for homeowners associations or HOA fees. You won't have to handle any HOA disputes by yourself, either.

Renting also offers greater mobility and freedom. Being a renter gives you the flexibility to move to a more convenient apartment if you change jobs or start a new relationship. Most leases are for one year, but you may find others with month-to-month arrangements if you need greater freedom. It means you can choose a new home in a desirable area for your commute, school, or shopping centers.

When you rent, you can enjoy financial stability against any market crashes. If the housing market crashes and property values significantly drop, you'll be unaffected. This also means you can enjoy the freedom to upsize or downsize to a different home if your needs change, regardless of current property values.

Renting can also be beneficial to your finances. Since it requires a smaller upfront financial commitment compared to buying a home, you can enjoy stable monthly costs as you'll have fewer unexpected expenses compared to homeownership.

Many rental properties are available furnished, so you won't have the expense of buying an entire home's worth of furniture. You also won't have the hassle of moving furniture if you live temporarily in an area or plan to move frequently.

Finally, if you rent an apartment, you may access added amenities such as community spaces, fitness centers, pools, and more at no additional cost. You may also have safety and security features, such as controlled access and surveillance systems, to protect your personal well-being.

The Advantages of Owning a Home with a Mortgage

While renting has many advantages, owning a home with a mortgage also has some distinct benefits.

The first thing that a mortgage can provide is control over your monthly payments, particularly if you have a fixed-rate mortgage. You won't be at the whim of a landlord and unexpected rent hikes.

You can also build equity in your home with every mortgage payment. It is almost like forced savings, as you increase your stake in the property.

Over time, the value of your house can be appreciated. Historically, property values tend to rise over time, which means there is the potential to get a significant return when you decide to sell.

You can also use the equity in your home to finance significant expenses like consolidating debt or making home improvements by taking out a home equity loan or line of credit. As we discussed earlier, this can provide a flexible form of financing at a lower rate since the lender has the property as collateral.

There are other benefits of paying a mortgage every month. Making timely mortgage payments helps improve your credit score. You may also access tax deductions on property taxes and mortgage interest, which might reduce your tax liabilities each year.

Although having a mortgage and owning a home is more of a responsibility, it offers some psychological benefits. When you own your home, you'll have the freedom to decorate, make changes, and even remodel without needing approval from a landlord. It means you can create a stable home for yourself and your family.

You may also feel a greater sense of community involvement. Since homeownership means you'll stay in one place longer, it helps you have stronger social connections, which can contribute to better physical and mental health.

Homeownership vs. Renting

Other benefits aside, for most people, the choice of owning a home vs. renting will come down to finances. Therefore, it is critical to make a financial comparison. Here's what you need to consider:

The Initial Costs

The first thing you need to think about is the initial costs. You will likely need the first and last month's rent plus a security deposit when renting. So, if the apartment you're considering is $1,000 per month, you will need about $3,000 as your initial costs. This might change based on your lease, but it's important to know that you'll have to save up some extra cash for it.

If you are buying a home, you will need a down payment and the funds to cover the closing costs of the sales process. Closing costs are typically 2% to 5% of the price of the home, and the minimum deposit will depend on the type of mortgage. However, as noted in our mortgage chapter, the bigger the down payment, the better rates you are likely to get.

Ongoing Costs

The ongoing costs for renters are relatively straightforward. You will pay your rent each month as per your rental agreement. It's also recommended that you have renters insurance, which tends to be more affordable than homeowner's insurance, as it only covers personal possessions and liability (Team, 2022).

The ongoing costs for homeowners are a little more involved. As a homeowner, you not only need to make your mortgage payment each month, but you'll also need to pay property taxes (depending on your state) and homeowner's insurance. Homeowners also need to cover any HOA fees for community maintenance and amenities.

Maintenance and Repair Costs

Homeowners are responsible for all the repairs and maintenance of the property. The estimated overall cost of repairs and maintenance can be approximately 1% of the property value per year for homeowners (Average Home Maintenance Costs, n.d.).

Renters have far less responsibility for maintenance. The landlord is generally responsible for all major repairs, but as a renter, your lease may specify that you are responsible for minor issues.

Equity vs. Rent Increases

As you make your mortgage payments each month, if the value of your property increases, more equity will be created in your home. Over time, this can make your home a significant financial asset. There is a potential to generate a profit when it comes time to sell your property.

On the other hand, landlords may increase the rent each year, subject to the location and the market conditions. If the property values in your preferred area have gone up, the chances are that rents will also increase.

Let Numbers Decide: A Quantitative Analysis

Now it's time to get into some math to help you decide about renting vs homeownership. Don't worry; there is only one formula to learn, so you don't need flashbacks to algebra class. You can also find online calculators that have this formula built in to make them easier for you.

This formula is useful as it helps you estimate the future appreciated value or the increased costs. We need to know the following elements before we can use this formula (Stevens, 2023).

1. Initial Value (e.g., current home value)
2. Annual Increase Rate (like interest rate or home value increase)
3. Number of Years

Future Value = Initial Value × (1+ Increase Rate)$^{\text{Number of Years}}$

Home Appreciation Estimates

To calculate how much your home value has the potential to increase, you can use the above formula and get an estimate. The annual increase rate can be determined by looking at local trends in the past. You can find this data on sites like Zillow and Redfin. However, keep in mind that previous performance does not guarantee future outcomes.

Property Tax

You can use the same formula to figure out how much property tax you'll have to pay in the long run. In this case, the initial value would be your starting property tax. We will see an example later in the chapter.

When searching for a new property to buy, remember to discuss the tax rates in the area with your realtor.

Maintenance and Insurance Costs

Insurance cost depends highly on the location. You can get quotes for coverage from potential providers. Also, as mentioned earlier, the general rule is to budget around 1% of the property value for maintenance.

Net Cost Comparison

To make a net cost comparison for buying a home, you'll need to take the estimated home value in year X minus the total mortgage interest payments, insurance, maintenance costs, cumulative property taxes, and additional fees.

For the cost of renting, you'll need to add up all the rental payments over the same period.

These calculations are fundamental, and there are some important caveats when making a cost comparison. For example, you may think about the opportunity cost of your down payment. Could you invest those funds elsewhere for a higher return than a down payment?

You also need to think about real estate in a local context. Historic local trends are far more accurate and relevant than national averages. Plus, different states have different property tax rates, regulations, and rent control laws that could affect your calculations.

Let's put these formulas into action with an example:

For a home with a purchase price of $300,000, we can estimate the home value in three years at $327,818.1, given an appreciation rate of 3% per year.

$$\text{Future Value} = (\$300,000) \times (1+0.03)^3 = \$327,818.1$$

So, the appreciated equity will be $27,818.1.

Let's assume we took a 30-year fixed-rate mortgage of 5% with a 20% down payment, which means we have $240,000 in debt. As you recall from the previous chapter, we pay more interest at the beginning of the mortgage. For the first three years, the breakdown between interest and principal payment would look like Table 8.1:

Year	Interest	Principal	Ending Balance
1	$11,919.59	$3,540.88	$236,459.12
2	$11,738.43	$3,722.03	$232,737.09
3	$11,548.00	$3,912.46	$228,824.63
Total	**$35,206.02**	**$11,175.37**	

Table 8.1 *The breakdown of principal and interest for the first three years of the loan.*

Let's assume that this property would have an initial property tax of $3,000 for the first year, and with a 2% annual increase, the total property tax would be $9,181.2.

1. **Year 1:** $3,000
2. **Year 2:** ($3,000) $\times$ $(1+0.02)^1$ =$3,060
3. **Year 3:** ($3,000) $\times$ $(1+0.02)^2$ =$3,121.2

There would also be maintenance costs of $3,000 in the first year based on the 1% rule and insurance costs of $1,000. Over three years, assuming a 2% increase per year, this could add up to a total of $12,241.6.

1. **Year 1:** $4,000
2. **Year 2:** ($4,000) $\times$ $(1+0.02)^1$ =$4,080
3. **Year 3:** ($4,000) $\times$ $(1+0.02)^2$ =$4,161.6

So, the total costs of home ownership over three years would approximately be:

$$\$35{,}206.02 + \$11{,}175.37 + \$9{,}181.2 + \$12{,}241.6 = \mathbf{\$67{,}804.19}$$

We need to subtract the house's equity to find the net cost.

Net Cost = $\$67{,}804.19 - (\$11{,}175.37 + \$27{,}818.1) = \mathbf{\$28{,}810.72}$

In comparison, if the current annual rent is $15,000 (including renter insurance) and there is a 3% annual increase over the same period, the total amount of rent paid would be $46,363.5

Year 1: $15,000

Year 2: $(\$15{,}000) \times (1+0.03)^1 = \mathbf{\$15{,}450}$

Year 3: $(\$15{,}000) \times (1+0.03)^2 = \mathbf{\$15{,}913.5}$

These calculations provide a basic comparison between renting and the potential costs of owning across three years. To make it even more accurate, you must exclude all the closing costs and realtor fees from the appreciation at the time of selling. You may also consider the potential tax deductions you get because of the mortgage interest.

In the above scenario, owning the house is more favorable than renting. However, notice that owning the house is more costly ($67,804.19 vs $46,363.5) and only makes sense when we consider the built-in equity.

Some Real-World Examples

Here are a few scenarios you might find relatable based on your financial circumstances. We'll go through different lifestyles and conditions to see if it makes sense for these people to rent or buy.

The Recent Graduate

Carlos is a 23-year-old recent graduate who landed his first job with a modest salary in Philadelphia. Carlos faces a tight financial situation because of his student loan. He chooses to rent a small studio apartment close to his new workplace. The affordability of renting and minimal maintenance and utility costs fit well into his budget.

Carlos aims to clear his student loan debt and establish a good credit score. In this situation, renting is financially prudent as it allows him to allocate a significant portion of his income towards repaying his debt without creating an additional financial burden of a mortgage, property taxes, or any unexpected home repairs. Renting also allows Carlos the flexibility to move if there is an opportunity for a better job or career progression.

Renting seems like the most viable option for Carlos to stabilize his finances.

The Young Professionals

Sarah is 24 and has recently landed her dream job in San Francisco after graduating. She's excited about her new tech career, but she knows the city has a notoriously high cost of living and the job market fluctuates. She has rented a small apartment near her job.

In this scenario, renting is advantageous. It provides Sarah with the flexibility that she needs during this stage of her life. Currently, she is unsure where her career will take her and wants to remain open to opportunities where she may need to relocate. Plus, for Sarah, the financial commitment of purchasing a home in San Francisco feels a bit intimidating. Sarah prefers to invest savings into a diversified stock portfolio with the potential for higher long-term returns.

By renting, Sarah can enjoy a vibrant city life without worrying about the fluctuating real estate market and the financial burden of maintenance costs and property taxes.

The Industrious Factory Worker

Emma has worked in a local factory in her small Midwest town for the last eight years. Now she's 28, she has accumulated some decent savings by living modestly, avoiding debt, and diligently budgeting. Her savings could provide a substantial down payment on a home.

In her town, homeownership costs, including mortgage payments, taxes, and insurance, are comparable or even lower than renting. Her area's housing market is stable but not rapidly appreciating, making it an affordable option. Emma decides to purchase a modest home she sees as a long-term investment. Her mortgage payments are within her financial means, and she sees the potential to build equity.

For Emma, buying is not only a financial decision but something that can provide an investment in her future stability.

The Early Career Success Story

At 29 years old, Emily has successfully settled down in her thriving small hometown. Since graduating from college, she has held the same job and was recently promoted. She feels confident about her career stability and decides to buy a home in her town because real estate is affordable and stable compared to larger cities. She has plans to stay in her hometown, and her mortgage payments are manageable and comparable to her previous rent, but she has the added benefit of being able to build equity.

For Emily, buying a home reflects her commitment to her community and is a sound financial decision.

The Young Entrepreneur

Alex is 30 and has launched his own start-up. He is based in a mid-sized city with a favorable real estate market. He has decided to buy a home and is eager to put down roots. Owning a home serves Alex as a personal accomplishment, along with his entrepreneurial ventures.

His new home doubles as his office, reducing initial business overhead costs. The property taxes and mortgage interest are partially tax deductible, so Alex views his new home as a dual investment for his personal life and business future.

Alex felt comfortable buying property because he wanted to stay in one place while his business grew, where he could join the local business community.

Final Thoughts

There are many variables when choosing between renting or buying a home, and every person's situation is different. Just because your friends bought a home or your colleagues rent doesn't mean it's the right decision for you. Apply the information you've learned and make the best choice for you and your future.

Our last chapter will focus on deciphering financial news and the commonly used jargon. It's all about staying informed and being open to learning.

Chapter 9

Making Sense of Financial News

"Let the views of others educate and inform you, but let your decisions be a product of your own conclusions." ~ Jim Rohn

They say information is power. Indeed, the more knowledge we have, the wiser choices we can make. Today's world lives and breathes information. Thanks to the internet, cable news, and social media, we can now stay updated to the minute.

But when it comes to financial news, there is so much going on that it's hard to keep up. Plus, things can get quite technical, making it challenging to understand key news and information. In particular, all those numbers and charts can get overwhelming. However, don't let the jargon intimidate you. In this chapter, we'll help you better understand financial news and articles so you can make sense of what you hear or read.

What Exactly Is Financial News?

Financial news refers to reporting on the economy, the stock market, business, and the overall financial world. News always comes in, giving you a health report of the country's economic system. Additionally, financial news offers detailed data on the world economy by regions such as Europe, Asia, or Latin America. Some news agencies specialize in certain regions, helping investors and the public stay on top of political, economic, and social developments.

Let's check out some of the most common news sections together.

Stock Market Updates

Financial news dedicates a fair chunk of airtime to the stock market. Major indices like the Dow Jones, S&P 500, and Nasdaq are the main benchmarks for evaluating stock market performance. These indices group publicly traded companies, allowing investors and the public to assess their performance. Here's a snapshot of what you can expect in each index:

- **Dow Jones:** The "Dow" tracks 30 large publicly traded companies in the United States. Apple, Microsoft, and other leading companies are part of the Dow Jones. Since 1896, the Dow has been the benchmark for the stock market in the United States and the world.

- **S&P 500:** The Standard and Poor's 500 is an index comprising 500 of the largest companies in the U.S. Companies like Tesla, Nvidia, and Berkshire Hathaway are part of this index.

- **Nasdaq:** The Nasdaq is heavily weighted toward technology and internet-based companies. This index often includes some of the fastest-growing companies in the market and from various sectors.

Stock market updates provide information on how well these indices are doing. Other international indices from Asia and Europe also receive considerable coverage. You can find plenty of up-to-date information on markets based in London (FTSE 100), Shanghai (SSE Composite Index), or Tokyo (Nikkei 225), among other critical international stock exchanges.

Corporate Earnings and News

One of the primary elements of financial reports is the coverage of companies' earnings quarterly or annually. It usually covers the companies' revenue, profit margins, and what their future looks like. For example, you would see headlines like *"Apple's Q2 Earnings beat the expectation."* (Q2 refers to the second quarter of the year) These types of news can affect the company's stock prices. As a shareholder, monitoring a company's earnings can provide valuable insights.

Along with financial news, major changes or decisions from big companies often grab attention. "Mergers and Acquisitions" is one example of a situation where different companies merge, or one company purchases another. Headlines like *"Company A acquires Company B for $10 billions"* are common for these types of news. Another example is when a company does some restructuring or lays off employees.

Economic Indicators

Economic indicators are a key component of financial news. Indicators such as Gross Domestic Product (GDP), inflation, or unemployment capture the headlines. The Department of Labor, The Bureau of Economic Analysis (BEA), and the Fed are among the agencies reporting some of these measures. You will often come across headlines such as *U.S. GDP Growth Slows to 2.3% in Q1 Amidst Rising Inflation.*

Cryptocurrency and Digital Assets

Despite the controversy, the media consistently covers cryptocurrency and its impact on the economy. The key reported metrics are usually the market capitalization (a.k.a. market cap) and the current price of the mainstream crypto like Bitcoin and Ethereum.

Market cap is a term used in both stocks and crypto. We can define Market Cap as (Fernando, 2024):

Market Cap = Current Stock/Crypto Price × Total Number of
Outstanding Shares/Tokens

Economic Policies and Government Actions

We learned how Federal Reserves and government decisions affect our daily finances. So, it's not surprising that they'd take up some of the financial news time and resources. Monetary Policies and Fiscal Policies are among the important topics covered by the media. Some examples are headlines like: *"Federal Reserve raised interest rates by 0.5% to combat the inflation."*

Why Is Financial News Important to Us?

Financial news applies to everyone. For instance, fluctuations in the stock market can have a significant impact on your investments or retirement accounts.

Keeping up with financial news provides insight into the state of the world, enabling you to make the best choices for your wallet. When the economy is good, you can make important purchases, such as a house. When financial news is not good, you may choose to wait longer to make an offer on that house.

Here are a few important ways financial news affects us.

Retirement Funds

Retirement accounts like 401(k) or pension plans frequently invest your contributions in stocks. So, if the stock market is doing well, your fund will do well, too. If the stock market is down, your fund may take a hit. That's why keeping tabs on financial news can help you assess your fund's situation. Depending on the situation, you can work with your financial advisor to find the best alternatives to help you ride out market downturns and cash in on upswings.

Job Security and Employment Opportunities

When employment data is positive, you can have greater confidence in the security of your job. You might even pursue other employment opportunities. However, when you hear about high unemployment numbers, job cuts, or companies losing money, you might want to reconsider your financial situation. While your employment may be stable, the broader economic climate implies that you must be cautious with your finances and maximize your savings.

Prices and Inflation

The Consumer Price Index (CPI) and inflation data are good indicators of the economy's performance. For example, when you hear inflation is rising month after month, you can expect the Fed to take some actions, like changing the interest rates.

Economic Policy

The government and Federal Reserve regularly update the public on economic policies. For example, hikes in interest rates can make getting a mortgage or a car loan more expensive. Similarly, tax increases can take a bite out of your paycheck. The following channels provide some of this data.

Federal Reserve

- **Federal Open Market Committee (FOMC) Statements:** The FOMC, which sets interest rates and conducts monetary policy, releases statements after each meeting summarizing its policy decisions and economic outlook. Financial news outlets widely cover these statements and can be found on the Federal Reserve Board's website (Federal Open Market Committee, n.d.).

- **Monetary Policy Reports:** The Fed publishes semi-annual Monetary Policy Reports to Congress that detail its economic forecasts and policy goals.

- **Public Speeches and Testimony:** Fed officials, including the Chair, frequently deliver speeches and participate in Congressional hearings, discussing economic conditions and policy considerations.

Other Government Agencies

- **The White House:** The White House releases statements and fact sheets outlining the administration's economic priorities and proposed policies. Press briefings and public addresses by the President may also address financial issues. You can find these on the White House website.

- **Department of the Treasury:** The Treasury Department issues reports and announcements on fiscal policy matters, including the federal budget, taxes, and government spending.

- **Bureau of Labor Statistics (BLS):** The BLS, a department within the Department of Labor, regularly releases key economic data reports. These reports include the monthly unemployment rate, jobs reports, and inflation data (Consumer Price Index). You can find them on the BLS website.

- **Congressional Hearings:** Committees in the U.S. Congress hold hearings to examine economic policy issues and receive testimony from government officials and financial experts. These hearings are often televised or live-streamed and can be a valuable source of information.

Financial News in Action

All right, reading financial articles can seem intimidating and boring. It's especially true when they're packed with jargon. That's why, in this section, I'll introduce you to some of the most common words and phrases you might come across in financial news or articles. Keep in mind that these stories are not real, but they are designed to make the concept easier to grasp.

Story 1: GDP and High-Level Macroeconomics

Recent data shows stagnant GDP growth along with lackluster consumer spending and exports, sparking stagflation concerns. Economists diligently track these indicators with concerns of prolonged economic stagnation and rising inflation.

GDP figures for the last quarter fell short of expectations, showing a slowdown in economic expansion. Analysts attribute this tepid growth to various factors, including supply chain disruptions, labor shortages, and wavering consumer confidence.

Consumer spending, a vital driver of economic activity, also showed signs of weakness. Despite fiscal attempts to boost demand, consumers remain cautious due to job insecurity and inflation concerns. This cautious approach has dampened retail sales and overall expenditure, further exacerbating the economic slowdown.

The combination of stagnant economic growth and rising inflationary pressures has raised concerns about stagflation – a scenario characterized by low growth and high inflation.

Let's break down a few important terms:

- **Macroeconomics:** A branch of economics that studies the overall economy from the big picture. It looks into variables like inflation, GDP, employment, etc. Conversely, **microeconomics** focuses on smaller players, like individuals and businesses.

- **GDP (Gross Domestic Product):** The value of the final products and services produced in the country, without including the intermediate goods and services used in their creation (Gross Domestic Product n.d.). In the U.S., they report GDP quarterly.

- **Consumer Spending:** Refers to the amount of money people spend on goods and services in a given period. Researchers usually calculate consumer spending monthly per household. Increasing consumer spending is a sign that people feel the economy is doing well, whereas falling or contracting consuming spending is a sign that people are worried about their economic future.

- **Stagflation:** An economic situation in which prices increase (higher inflation) with little or no economic growth (stagnant economy) and high unemployment.

Story 2: Stock Market

This week, the Dow Jones Industrial Average experienced a surge because of gains from blue-chip companies. Despite initial worries about market volatility, investors stayed bullish, causing the index to rise significantly. Blue-chip stalwarts such as Apple, Microsoft, and Johnson & Johnson led the charge posted robust earnings.

The Dow's upward trend signifies a growing assurance of the market's stability and the underlying power of these industry giants. Analysts credit the positive sentiment to encouraging economic indicators and solid corporate performance. However, concerns linger regarding ongoing geopolitical tensions and the potential impact of inflationary pressures. Investors closely watch earnings reports and central bank policies as they navigate market volatility.

Even with the unpredictable nature of the market, the prevailing optimism emphasizes the lasting appeal of blue-chip investments in today's volatile landscape.

Here are the important terms to check:

- **Blue-Chip Companies:** A blue-chip company is a publicly traded company that is financially stable and well-established. They have gained a reputation for their widely recognized products and services. Typically, these companies have a high market capitalization and a proven profitability and growth track record. Some examples are Coca-Cola, McDonald's, and IBM (Chen, 2024).

- **Bullish Market:** In short, a "Bullish" market means investors have confidence that stock prices will grow in the future. On the flip side, investors refer to the opposite of this condition as a "Bearish" market.

- **Market Volatility:** Volatility is the term used to describe the fluctuations in the market. Volatility is perfectly normal. However, unexpected fluctuations may signal something is wrong. For instance, unfavorable economic data, like a very high inflation report, may lead to wild swings in stock prices.

Story 3: Real Estate Market Dynamics

Housing demand is surging in a growing seller's market. The restricted housing inventory increases the potential for Real Estate Investment Trusts (REITs). As homebuyers face fierce competition and limited options, REITs are poised to capitalize on this trend.

Sellers benefit from low mortgage rates and a lack of available properties, giving them more leverage in negotiations and increasing prices. This factor boosts the profitability of REITs and underscores their ability to thrive in volatile economic conditions.

Investors are eyeing REITs as a strategic avenue to gain exposure to the booming real estate sector without the complexities of property ownership. By pooling resources into diversified portfolios of income-generating properties, REITs offer investors a passive income stream and potential capital appreciation in a thriving market.

With no signs of slowing down housing demand and limited housing inventory, REITs are an attractive investment option that can generate strong returns in the coming months.

Here's a look at the important terms:

- **Housing Demand:** People's desire to own homes within a specific region and period.

- **Housing Inventory:** The total number of residential properties available for sale within a specific region and period.

- **Seller's Market:** A condition when there are fewer homes available for sale. Therefore, buyers compete with one another, often raising prices. The opposite of this situation is "Buyer's Market," which is favorable to buyers.

- **Real Estate Investment Trusts (REITs):** A REIT is a company that owns and typically runs income-generating real estate or related assets. For example, they buy apartments, hotels, and warehouses and rent them out to generate income. Their shares are typically available for purchase on major stock exchanges (Real Estate Investment Trusts (REITs) | Investor.gov, n.d.).

Story 4: Fiscal Policy and Its Impacts

Governments worldwide are reconsidering their approaches as debates on the role of fiscal policy in economic growth and income inequality continue. With economies grappling with the aftermath of the pandemic, attention is turning to the efficacy of fiscal stimuli.

While government spending remains a crucial tool, concerns persist regarding its impact on national deficits. Tax policies are under scrutiny, with calls for progressive reforms to address income inequality. The challenge lies in balancing growth objectives with social equity.

In response, policymakers are reevaluating fiscal policies, seeking to optimize outcomes. Strategies are being tailored to promote sustainable growth while mitigating inequality.

Let's discuss the key points:

- **Fiscal Policy:** Refers to the government's utilization of spending and taxation to shape the economy. Governments usually use fiscal policy to boost growth and reduce poverty (Fiscal Policy: Taking and Giving Away, 2019).

- **Economic Growth:** It refers to the growth in the production of goods and services from one period to another (Team, 2024). Economic growth is a sign that the economy is healthy. The Bureau of Economic Analysis (BEA) measures the GDP as the primary growth indicator (Who Measures GDP, n.d.).

- **Government Spending:** This is the money that the government spends on all goods and services. This includes infrastructure, social programs, education, national defense, law enforcement and public safety, scientific research, national parks and recreation areas.

- **Tax Policies:** These policies are the laws and regulations set forth by Congress and signed by the President. They determine how the government sets, collects, and manages taxes.

- **National Deficit:** The deficit is the money the government has spent more than its revenue. For example, in the fiscal year 2023, the U.S. government spent $6.13 trillion and received $4.44 trillion in revenue. Basically, they spent an extra $1.7 trillion, also known as deficit spending (Fiscal Data Explains the National Deficit, n.d.). The fiscal year in the U.S. government starts on October 1 and ends on September 30 (The Federal Budget Process | USAGov, n.d.).

- **Fiscal Stimulus:** This policy generally encourages economic growth through more government spending and tax cuts. The goal is to encourage investment and spending, increasing household income and business investments.

Story 5: The Rise of Rollover, Self-Directed, and SIMPLE IRAs in Retirement Planning

The retirement savings environment is experiencing significant shifts as more and more people opt for rollover IRAs, self-directed IRAs, and SIMPLE IRAs. You can customize your retirement planning to fit your situation because there are many options to choose from that match different financial goals and investment preferences.

If you're an investor, consider these IRA options and how they can benefit your retirement portfolio. If you plan to open an IRA, assess how each type fits your retirement goals and chat with a financial consultant for advice.

- **Rollover IRA:** A great option for those transitioning careers permitting the transfer of retirement funds from an employer plan like 401K to an IRA. It provides investors additional investment choices while maintaining tax deferral for their capital (Rollover

Old 401(K)S Into IRAs With Schwab, n.d.).

- **Self-Directed IRA:** Allows people to diversify their retirement portfolios by adding alternative assets such as real estate, precious metals, or commodities. If you want direct control over your retirement assets, this type of IRA is worth considering (Folger, 2024).

- **SIMPLE IRA:** Great choice for small business owners and their teams (usually less than 100 employees). This plan simplifies the process of opening a retirement savings account with employer contributions and tax-deferral benefits (SIMPLE IRA Plan, n.d.). If you start your own business and hire employees, this would be a great option for their benefits.

Story 6: Understanding IPO Options

We are witnessing more and more businesses choosing to go public through SPACs and traditional IPOs. Although the IPO market is undergoing major changes, there are many ways for investors to enter the markets, and each can fulfill a certain set of objectives and tastes. Investors should explore these IPO possibilities as they give them a chance to engage with start-ups while diversifying their investment portfolios. While an IPO can be a great investment, it often poses more risks, so do your due diligence and get professional advice if needed.

- **Due Diligence:** In simple terms, due diligence involves performing a comprehensive investigation, audit, or review to validate the facts and details associated with a matter that is being considered. In finance, before entering into a proposed transaction with someone, it is necessary to perform due diligence by examining financial records (Chen, 2024).

- **Going Public:** This is the process of making a company's privately held shares available to new investors. It is also called an initial public offering or, in short, IPO (Chen, 2023).

- **Traditional IPO:** In a traditional IPO, private companies raise capital by selling new shares to investment banks (underwriters), who then sell them primarily to institutional investors (SEC.gov | IPO, a SPAC, And a Direct Listing, 2022).

- **SPAC (Special Purpose Acquisition Company):** SPACs are companies that exist solely to merge with or buy another existing company (Young, 2023). Imagine you have a thriving technology startup that aims to go public. However, the traditional IPO process is lengthy and requires navigating many regulatory hurdles. A SPAC, which is essentially a shell company listed on the stock market, contacts you to propose a merger. This SPAC merger will let your startup go public.

Final Thoughts

Ultimately, financial reports are no different from other types of news. They share the latest information with the public, like sports, entertainment, or politics. Similarly, they are not immune to bias. That is why it is vital to rely on multiple credible sources and come to your own conclusions.

Building a Brighter Future Together

"The best way to predict the future is to create it." - Peter Drucker

We all have experienced those moments of great joy and accomplishment when we finally reached one of our goals. But have you ever wished "If only someone had guided me sooner"? We're always striving to better our lives and the lives of those we care about. Now, consider the possibilities of expediting this process by gaining knowledge from the insights and experiences of others. It would enable us to avoid typical mistakes and accomplish our goals faster and more effectively.

I wrote this book to be that guiding voice and to share the knowledge and skills I've learned. Being financially literate can make all the difference in the world, especially for younger adults. Nevertheless, any book will only have an impact if it reaches its target audience.

This is where your help can make an enormous impact. If you have found this book informative and helpful, please consider leaving an honest review. This will help others find this resource more easily and become more confident in riding their financial rollercoaster.

Before we move on to the Conclusion, I want to take a moment to thank you for reading and reviewing this book. Together, we can build a brighter and prosperous future.

Conclusion

And that's all he wrote! You may have come to the end of this book, but your journey to financial literacy is far from over; in fact, it's only just begun. It's up to you to take everything you've learned here and apply it to your life and finances. Whether your goal is to save more money, qualify for a mortgage or an auto loan, improve your credit score, or ride out tough times during a recession and inflation, you can consider yourself educated and empowered to do so. (And don't worry if you're still uncertain about things—this book is here to stand as a reference whenever you need a refresher.)

When I was young, I didn't have much of a formal financial 'education.' I knew that saving money was a good thing (obviously), but I didn't know the best way to do that. I vaguely knew that recessions, deflation, and inflation could damage my finances, but I wasn't quite sure of the details. I also knew my credit score was important to my financial health, but again, I was not clued in on many details. That's the driving force behind this book; I wanted to share what I've learned over the years to ensure you don't face the same pitfalls I did. If I'd had a book like this when I was trying to build my wealth and manage my finances, I would have been able to make more informed decisions and avoid a lot of pain points.

That's what it all comes down to, in the end. Making choices that positively impact your finances and, ultimately, your quality of life. It's tough to manage what you don't understand. That's why we began with a discussion on inflation and deflation in an attempt to demystify this often misunderstood economic phenomenon. When you know the underlying conditions that lead to inflation and deflation, you can better manage your money when the broader economy is in the midst of these states. That discussion went further in Chapter 3 with an explanation of recessions and how to not only survive but appropriately manage your finances to thrive during them.

We tackled the Federal Reserve in Chapter 4. While it might not be the world's most fascinating topic, knowing how the Federal Reserve works built a foundation for understanding Chapter 5's lessons on loans and borrowing. Knowing what the Federal Reserve is up to when raising and lowering interest rates is a great way to make better decisions before taking out any large loans. When the rates are high, you might want to hold off on that new car or new house until things start to come down. Although it may delay your purchases in the short term, you'll save a lot of money in the long run.

Chapter 6 emphasized the significant impact of credit cards on our personal finances. Responsible use of credit is key to building a healthy credit history and score. The key word here is 'Responsible.' Doing your research when choosing cards to apply for goes a long way toward having a line of credit that works FOR you, not against you. Interest rates and perks are important, but paying your bill on time and in full whenever possible is also essential. And *always, always, always* read the terms and conditions and make sure you understand them before signing anything!

Home buying and mortgages are such huge chunks of financial health that we took two whole chapters to discuss them. Purchasing a home is likely the largest purchase you make in your lifetime, so minding your credit score and waiting for the best rates is critical to getting the most bang for your buck. And if you decide you'll never buy a house, that's okay, too! This is your financial journey, and you get to make the decisions that make the most sense for you.

I finished the book with information on how to digest financial news. Being able to read, watch, and interpret financial happenings can help you meet and exceed your needs and goals. It's a continuous learning cycle that keeps you learning and growing your knowledge and wealth.

Ultimately, your goal is to live a comfortable life, be financially prepared for any downturns, and have access to the necessary information to make informed decisions about your financial well-being.

I know it can all be a little intimidating. I understand the fear of job uncertainty or the panic of being too broke to get my car fixed. It can happen to anyone, so it's always best to be prepared. I hope this book was able to ease some of your fears.

Now, it's time for you to write your own financial story. Remember that you're not only more prepared for challenges ahead; you have the tools and knowledge to conquer them. Be diligent, do your research, keep those credit scores high, and stay on top of the financial news and trends. Get out there and make your mark. Your journey on the road of financial literacy is just starting, and the future is bright!

References

14 Mortgage Questions to Ask Your Lender. (n.d.). NerdWallet. https://www.nerdwallet.com/article/mortgages/mortgage-questions-and-answers

30 year fixed mortgage: Pros, Cons & Comparison calculator. (2023, April 13). Debt.org. https://www.debt.org/real-estate/mortgages/30-year-fixed/

4.4 Loan origination fees and costs. (n.d.). Viewpoint.pwc.com. https://viewpoint.pwc.com/dt/us/en/pwc/accounting_guides/loans_and_investment/loans_and_investment_US/chapter_4_accounting__1_US/4 4_loan_origination__US.html#pwc-topic.dita_1604305510040130

5 Ways to Bolster Your Finances in a Recession | Morgan Stanley. (2023). Morgan Stanley. https://www.morganstanley.com/articles/managing-finances-during-recession

6 Ways to Pay Off Your Mortgage Early - Nationwide. (n.d.). https://www.nationwide.com/lc/resources/home/articles/pay-off-mortgage-faster

7 Ways to Recession-Proof Your Life. (n.d.). Investopedia. https://www.investopedia.com/articles/pf/08/recession-proof-your-life.asp

Agbaje. (2023, October 31). What happens when a government prints money? | American bullion. American Bullion - Gold IRA. https://www.americanbullion.com/what-happens-when-a-government-prints-money/

Akin, J. (2023, July 29). What affects your credit scores? https://www.experian.com/blogs/ask-experian/credit-education/score-basics/what-affects-your-credit-scores/

Amortization calculator. (n.d.).
https://www.calculator.net/amortization-calculator.html

An Update on Emerging Issues in Banking How Real is the Threat of
Deflation to the Banking Industry? (2003).
https://www.fdic.gov/analysis/archived-research/fyi/022703fyi.pdf

Andrew Bloomenthal. (n.d.). The Better Inflation Hedge: Gold or
Treasuries? Investopedia.
https://www.investopedia.com/articles/investing/092514/better-
inflation-hedge-gold-or-treasuries.asp

Annual Credit Report.com - Home Page. (2019).
Annualcreditreport.com.
https://www.annualcreditreport.com/index.action

Appendix KK FRB In Plain English Brochure. (n.d.). Retrieved
February 16, 2024, from
https://www.federalreserve.gov/pubs/oss/oss3/ssbf03/append_KK/37Ap
pendixKK_FRB_Plain_English_Brochure.pdf

Araj, V. (n.d.). Mortgage Rate lock: A guide to protect you from rate
fluctuations. https://www.rocketmortgage.com/learn/mortgage-rate-
lock

Ashford, K. (2020, August 25). What Is Deflation? Forbes Advisor.
https://www.forbes.com/advisor/investing/what-is-deflation/

Author, B. (2021, June 16). An update on how households are using
stimulus checks - Liberty Street Economics. Liberty Street Economics.
https://libertystreeteconomics.newyorkfed.org/2021/04/an-update-on-
how-households-are-using-stimulus-checks/

Average home maintenance costs. (n.d.). American Family Insurance.
https://www.amfam.com/resources/articles/at-home/average-home-
maintenance-costs

A-Z Quotes | Quotes for All Occasions. (2019). A-Z Quotes.
https://www.azquotes.com

B3-3.1-01, General Income Information (12/13/2023). (2023). Fanniemae.com. https://selling-guide.fanniemae.com/Selling-Guide/Origination-thru-Closing/Subpart-B3-Underwriting-Borrowers/Chapter-B3-3-Income-Assessment/Section-B3-3-1-Employment-and-Other-Sources-of-Income/1032992031/B3-3-1-01-General-Income-Information-09-06-2023.htm

Baldwin, J. G. (2023, May 26). The Impact of a Fed Interest Rate Hike. Investopedia. https://www.investopedia.com/articles/investing/010616/impact-fed-interest-rate-hike.asp

Bell, D. N. F., & Blanchflower, D. G. (2011). Young People and the Great Recession. SSRN Electronic Journal. https://doi.org/10.2139/ssrn.1835313

Bell, L. (2024, April 9). What is a closing disclosure? Bankrate. https://www.bankrate.com/mortgages/closing-disclosure/

Bennett, K. (2023, May 1). What Is A Bank Bailout? Bankrate. https://www.bankrate.com/banking/what-is-a-bank-bailout

BLS Data Viewer. (n.d.). Beta.bls.gov. Retrieved February 16, 2024, from https://beta.bls.gov/dataViewer/view/timeseries/APU0000702111

Board of Governors of the Federal Reserve System. (2021, July 29). Federal Reserve Board - Monetary Policy: What Are Its Goals? How Does It Work? Board of Governors of the Federal Reserve System. https://www.federalreserve.gov/monetarypolicy/monetary-policy-what-are-its-goals-how-does-it-work.htm

BrainyQuote. (2019). BrainyQuote; BrainyQuote. https://www.brainyquote.com/quotes

Buczynski, B., & Wood, K. (2024, March 28). Conventional loan requirements for 2024. NerdWallet. https://www.nerdwallet.com/article/mortgages/conventional-loan-requirements-guidelines

References

Buying a Home | HUD.gov / U.S. Department of Housing and Urban Development (HUD). (n.d.). Www.hud.gov. https://www.hud.gov/topics/buying_a_home

By The Currency editors. (n.d.). What is deflation? Empower. https://www.empower.com/the-currency/money/deflation

By. (2021, August 25). 4 Ways to Avoid Credit Card Late Fees. Www.experian.com. https://www.experian.com/blogs/ask-experian/ways-to-avoid-credit-card-late-fees/

By. (2023, May 28). How Is a Credit Card Minimum Payment Calculated? - Experian. Www.experian.com. https://www.experian.com/blogs/ask-experian/how-is-your-credit-card-minimum-payment-calculated

Carnevale, A. P., Rose, S. J., Cheah, B., & THE GEORGETOWN UNIVERSITY CENTER ON EDUCATION AND THE WORKFORCE. (n.d.). Education, occupations, lifetime earnings. In THE GEORGETOWN UNIVERSITY CENTER ON EDUCATION AND THE WORKFORCE. https://cew.georgetown.edu/wp-content/uploads/2014/11/collegepayoff-complete.pdf

Cash, K. (2021, July 20). Credit Card vs. Debit: Which is Safer Online? NerdWallet. https://www.nerdwallet.com/article/credit-cards/credit-card-vs-debit-card-safer-online-purchases

CEPF®, T. T., BSc. (n.d.). Liquidity | Meaning, Significance, Types, Measures, Management. Finance Strategists. https://www.financestrategists.com/wealth-management/stocks/liquidity/

Cfp, H. M. B., & Metzger, P. (2024, May 6). 14 mortgage questions to ask your lender — and the answers you want. NerdWallet. https://www.nerdwallet.com/article/mortgages/mortgage-questions-and-answers?ajs_uid=bd6742c0ea82aeb20976ab2a6f7857a73699f9dcc3fc5c01e74c805aae9411d1®_gate_return=true

Chen, J. (2019). *Treasury inflation-protected securities protect investors from inflation*. Investopedia. https://www.investopedia.com/terms/t/tips.asp

Chen, J. (2024, January 18). *Due diligence*. Investopedia. https://www.investopedia.com/terms/d/duediligence.asp

Chen, J. (2024, May 9). *Blue chip meaning and examples*. Investopedia. https://www.investopedia.com/terms/b/bluechip.asp

COINNEWS MEDIA GROUP LLC. (2019, May 10). *U.S. Inflation Calculator*. U.S. Inflation Calculator. https://www.usinflationcalculator.com/

College Students Lacking Basic Credit Card Knowledge - CreditCardReviews.com. (n.d.). Www.creditcardreviews.com. https://www.creditcardreviews.com/blog/college-students-lacking-basic-credit-card-knowledge

Consumer Financial Protection Bureau. (2023, October 12). *Consumer Financial Protection Bureau*. https://www.consumerfinance.gov/ask-cfpb/what-can-i-do-if-i-think-a-mortgage-lender-discriminated-against-me-en-342/

Consumer Price Index Frequently asked questions. (2024, March 15). Bureau of Labor Statistics. https://www.bls.gov/cpi/questions-and-answers.htm

Crace, M. (2024, April 11). *What's a good credit score to buy a house?* Quicken Loans. https://www.quickenloans.com/learn/credit-score-to-buy-a-house

Credit inquiry. (2021, May 4). Experian. https://www.experian.com/blogs/ask-experian/credit-education/report-basics/hard-vs-soft-inquiries-on-your-credit-report/

Cussen, M. (2019). *What's the Difference Between Credit Cards and Debit Cards?* Investopedia. https://www.investopedia.com/articles/personal-finance/050214/credit-

vs-debit-cards-which-better.asp

Debt In America: Statistics and Demographics. (n.d.). Debt.org. Retrieved February 16, 2024, from https://www.debt.org/faqs/americans-in-debt/demographics

Debt.org - America's Debt Help Organization. (n.d.). Debt.org. http://www.debt.org/

Dehan, A. (2024, April 2). What is a jumbo loan and when do you need one? Bankrate. https://www.bankrate.com/mortgages/what-is-jumbo-mortgage/#how-it-works

Dehan, A. (2024, May 2). Conventional loans: What they are and how they work. Bankrate. https://www.bankrate.com/mortgages/what-is-a-conventional-loan/#comparison

Dellinger, A. (2024, March 11). Should you buy a house during a recession? Bankrate. https://www.bankrate.com/real-estate/buying-home-during-recession/#prices

DeNicola, L. (2019, December 4). When do late payments get reported? Experian. https://www.experian.com/blogs/ask-experian/when-do-late-payments-get-reported/

DeNicola, L. (2022, April 30). What is a billing cycle? Experian. https://www.experian.com/blogs/ask-experian/what-is-billing-cycle/

Department of Veterans Affairs. (n.d.). VA.gov | Veterans Affairs. https://www.benefits.va.gov/homeloans/

DeSilver, D. (2018, August 7). For most U.S. workers, real wages have barely budged in decades. Pew Research Center. https://www.pewresearch.org/short-reads/2018/08/07/for-most-us-workers-real-wages-have-barely-budged-for-decades/

Devaney, T. (2023, April 4). Hard credit inquiry vs. soft credit inquiry: What they are and why they matter. Intuit Credit Karma. https://www.creditkarma.com/advice/i/hard-credit-inquiries-and-soft-credit-inquiries

References

Dieker, N. (2022, September 20). *Credit Card vs Debit Card: Which Is Safer? Bankrate.* https://www.bankrate.com/finance/credit-cards/credit-card-vs-debit-card/#use

Dieker, N. (2023, October 25). *Guide to credit card minimum payments. Bankrate.* https://www.bankrate.com/finance/credit-cards/guide-to-credit-card-minimum-payments/#what

Dieker, N. (n.d.). *Everything You Need To Know About Credit Utilization Ratio. Bankrate.* https://www.bankrate.com/finance/credit-cards/credit-utilization-ratio/#affect

Different kinds of loans. (n.d.). *Consumer Financial Protection Bureau.* https://www.consumerfinance.gov/owning-a-home/explore/understand-the-different-kinds-of-loans-available/

Dollarhide, M. (2024, February 28). *What is an FHA mortgage insurance premium? Bankrate.* https://www.bankrate.com/mortgages/fha-mortgage-insurance-guide/#example

Douglas, L., & Douglas, L. (2023, April 21). *U.S. food banks warn of strain as Republicans seek food aid cuts. Reuters.* https://www.reuters.com/world/us/us-food-banks-warn-strain-republicans-seek-food-aid-cuts-2023-04-21/

Drenik, G. (n.d.). *How To Survive Deflation: The Impending Reality About To Hit Retailers. Forbes.* Retrieved February 16, 2024, from https://www.forbes.com/sites/garydrenik/2023/06/01/how-to-survive-deflation-the-impending-reality-about-to-hit-retailers/

Economics of Inflation - the Wage-Price-Spiral. (n.d.). *Reference Library | Economics | Tutor2u.* https://www.tutor2u.net/economics/reference/economics-of-inflation-the-wage-price-spiral

Edwards, E. (2023, May 2). *How Does A Recession Affect Your Personal Finances? PocketSmith.*

References

https://www.pocketsmith.com/blog/how-does-a-recession-affect-your-personal-finances

Equifax. (2023). Understanding hard inquiries on your credit report. Equifax. https://www.equifax.com/personal/education/credit/report/articles/-/learn/understanding-hard-inquiries-on-your-credit-report/

Federal Open Market Committee. (n.d.). https://www.federalreserve.gov/monetarypolicy/fomc.htm

Federal Reserve 2009 (n.d.). docshare.tips. https://docshare.tips/federal-reserve-2009_5820063cb6d87f6f998b4833.html

Federal Reserve Payments Study (FRPS). (n.d.). Www.federalreserve.gov. https://www.federalreserve.gov/paymentsystems/fr-payments-study.htm

Federal Reserve System | USAGOV. (n.d.). https://www.usa.gov/agencies/federal-reserve-system

Federal Reserve. (2019). Federal Reserve Board - About the Fed. Federalreserve.gov. https://www.federalreserve.gov/aboutthefed.htm

Fernando, J. (2019). What the Annual Percentage Rate – APR Tells You. Investopedia. https://www.investopedia.com/terms/a/apr.asp

Fernando, J. (2023, August 14). What is a debt security? Definition, types, and how to invest. Investopedia. https://www.investopedia.com/terms/d/debtsecurity.asp

Fernando, J. (2024, March 5). Market Capitalization: What it means for investors. Investopedia. https://www.investopedia.com/terms/m/marketcapitalization.asp

FHA Adjustable Rate Mortgage - HUD. (n.d.). HUD.gov / U.S. Department of Housing And Urban Development (HUD). https://www.hud.gov/program_offices/housing/sfh/ins/203armt

119

References

FHA Loan. (n.d.). CMG Financial. https://www.cmgfi.com/loan-programs/fha-loan

Fiscal data explains the national deficit. (n.d.). https://fiscaldata.treasury.gov/americas-finance-guide/national-deficit/

Fiscal policy: taking and giving away. (2019, June 28). IMF. https://www.imf.org/en/Publications/fandd/issues/Series/Back-to-Basics/Fiscal-Policy

Folger, J. (2024, March 4). Self-Directed IRA (SDIRA): Rules, investments, and FAQs. Investopedia. https://www.investopedia.com/terms/s/self-directed-ira.asp

Fontinelle, A. (2020, August 5). Average House Price by State in 2020 | The Ascent. The Motley Fool. https://www.fool.com/the-ascent/research/average-house-price-state/

Frankel, A. (2024, May 23). What is inflation? (2024). https://www.marketwatch.com/guides/banking/what-is-inflation/

George, D. (2021, February 10). How to Negotiate Loan Fees | The Motley Fool. Www.fool.com. https://www.fool.com/the-ascent/personal-loans/negotiate-fees/

Gibson, K., & Picchi, A. (2022, February 3). Starbucks to raise prices, blaming inflation. It's the third price hike since October. Www.cbsnews.com. https://www.cbsnews.com/news/starbucks-prices-inflation/

Gillespie, L. (2023, February 23). Bankrate's annual emergency fund report. Bankrate. https://www.bankrate.com/banking/savings/emergency-savings-report/

Goff, K. (n.d.). APR Vs. Interest Rate: What's The Difference? Bankrate. Retrieved February 16, 2024, from https://www.bankrate.com/mortgages/apr-and-interest-rate/#apr

Graham, K. (n.d.). A guide to loan estimates (Or "Good faith estimates"). https://www.rocketmortgage.com/learn/good-faith-

estimate

Green, D. (2024, May 21). USDA Loans | Requirement, map & Income Limits 2024. Mortgage Rates, Mortgage News and Strategy?: The Mortgage Reports. https://themortgagereports.com/14969/usda-loans-home-mortgage

Gross domestic product (n.d.). https://www.bea.gov/data/gdp/gross-domestic-product

Habits, B. M. (2023, August 9). What is APR? Types of credit card APR & how it's calculated. Better Money Habits. https://bettermoneyhabits.bankofamerica.com/en/credit/what-is-apr

Hawley, R. (2024, April 2). Car depreciation: What it is and how it works. Bankrate. https://www.bankrate.com/insurance/car/understanding-car-depreciation/

Hayes, A. (2021, July 25). What Are Some Examples of Common Credit Card Reward Program Benefits? Investopedia. https://www.investopedia.com/ask/answers/110614/what-are-some-examples-common-credit-card-reward-program-benefits.asp

Hayes, A. (2024, February 28). What are open market operations (OMOs), and how do they work? Investopedia. https://www.investopedia.com/terms/o/openmarketoperations.asp

Henry Ford quotes. (n.d.). BrainyQuote. https://www.brainyquote.com/quotes/henry_ford_136294

Here's Proof That Stocks Were Never an Inflation Hedge. (2023, February 24). Institutional Investor. https://www.institutionalinvestor.com/article/2bstowq7rxui2ct2sy4n4/portfolio/heres-proof-that-stocks-were-never-an-inflation-hedge

History not repeating: Why today's housing market won't turn into 2008's. (2021, May 3). Zillow Research. https://www.zillow.com/research/sustainable-housing-demand-2021-

not-2008-29424/

History of U.S. Treasury bills— TreasuryDirect. (n.d.).
https://www.treasurydirect.gov/research-center/history-of-marketable-
securities/bills

History: Handbook of Methods: U.S. Bureau of Labor Statistics. (n.d.).
Www.bls.gov. https://www.bls.gov/opub/hom/cpi/history.htm

House, W. (2022, July 26). How do economists determine whether the
economy is in a recession? The White House.
https://www.whitehouse.gov/cea/written-materials/2022/07/21/how-do-
economists-determine-whether-the-economy-is-in-a-recession

How Do Credit Card Issuers Calculate Minimum Payments? – Forbes
Advisor. (n.d.). Www.forbes.com.
https://www.forbes.com/advisor/credit-cards/how-do-credit-card-
issuers-calculate-minimum-payments/

How Does the Federal Reserve Interest Rate Affect Me? | Discover.
(2019, September 4). Discover Bank - Banking Topics Blog.
https://www.discover.com/online-banking/banking-topics/how-does-
the-federal-reserve-interest-rate-affect-me/

How Interest Rate Changes Affect Your Student Loans. (n.d.).
NerdWallet. https://www.nerdwallet.com/article/loans/student-
loans/fed-rate-hike-student-loans

How much does the average person make in a lifetime? (n.d.).
Www.zippia.com. https://www.zippia.com/answers/how-much-does-the-
average-person-make-in-a-lifetime/

How Much Down Payment Do You Need to Buy a Home? (2023,
September 24). NerdWallet.
https://www.nerdwallet.com/article/mortgages/how-much-down-
payment-for-house

How to Pick the Best Credit Card for You: 4 Easy Steps. (n.d.).
NerdWallet. https://www.nerdwallet.com/article/credit-cards/how-to-

pick-the-best-credit-card-for-you-4-easy-steps

Inflation of 2 percent (n.d.). Board of Governors of the Federal Reserve System. https://www.federalreserve.gov/faqs/economy_14400.htm

Interest rate and the APR. (2024, January 30). Consumer Financial Protection Bureau. https://www.consumerfinance.gov/ask-cfpb/what-is-the-difference-between-a-loan-interest-rate-and-the-apr-en-733/

International Monetary Fund. (2023, January). Monetary Policy and Central Banking. International Monetary Fund. https://www.imf.org/en/About/Factsheets/Sheets/2023/monetary-policy-and-central-banking

Jack Kemp quotes. (n.d.). BrainyQuote. https://www.brainyquote.com/authors/jack-kemp-quotes

Jain, A. (2020, September 25). Order of Liquidity. WallStreetMojo. https://www.wallstreetmojo.com/order-of-liquidity/

Jim Rohn quotes. (n.d.). BrainyQuote. https://www.brainyquote.com/quotes/jim_rohn_121282

Johnston, M. (2021, September 9). Breaking Down the Federal Reserve's Dual Mandate. Investopedia. https://www.investopedia.com/articles/investing/100715/breaking-down-federal-reserves-dual-mandate.asp

Kagan, J. (2019). Credit Score. Investopedia. https://www.investopedia.com/terms/c/credit_score.asp

Kagan, J. (2019, June 25). Grace period (Credit): What it is, how it works. Investopedia. https://www.investopedia.com/terms/g/grace-period-credit.asp

Kagan, J. (2021, February 25). Mortgage. Investopedia. https://www.investopedia.com/terms/m/mortgage.asp

Kagan, J. (n.d.). What Is Mortgage Insurance? Investopedia. https://www.investopedia.com/terms/m/mortgage-insurance.asp

References

Kastrenakes, J. (2019, March 18). *How phones went from $200 to $2,000. The Verge; The Verge.* https://www.theverge.com/2019/3/18/18263584/why-phones-are-so-expensive-price-apple-samsung-google

Kenton, W. (n.d.). *What Are Usury Laws? Investopedia.* https://www.investopedia.com/terms/u/usury-laws.asp

L. S. (2017, August 10). *17 Benefits Of Renting an Apartment. Market Apartments.* https://www.marketapts.com/blog/benefits-to-renting/

LabLynx. (2022, February 15). *Delta-8-THC: Delta-9-THC's nicer younger sibling? LiMSforum.com - the Global Laboratory, Informatics, Medical and Science Professional Community.* https://www.limsforum.com/delta-8-thc-delta-9-thcs-nicer-younger-sibling/101061/?rdp_we_resource=http%3A%2F%2Fen.wikipedia.org%2Fwiki%2FFederal_Reserve

Lake, R. (2023). *Loan Terms Explained. Investopedia.* https://www.investopedia.com/loan-terms-5075341

Luhby, T. (2018, May 24). *Many college grads from the Great Recession are still trying to catch up. CNNMoney.* https://money.cnn.com/2018/05/24/news/economy/great-recession-college-graduates/index.html

Maps of the Federal Reserve System. (n.d.). https://www.federalreserve.gov/boarddocs/rptcongress/annual07/pdf/maps.pdf

Marcos, C. M. (2022, February 1). *Starbucks will raise prices again, citing higher costs for supplies and workers. The New York Times.* https://www.nytimes.com/2022/02/01/business/starbucks-prices.html

Marks, C. (2023, August 23). *Inflation, Disinflation and Deflation: What Do They All Mean? Www.stlouisfed.org.* https://www.stlouisfed.org/open-vault/2023/august/explaining-inflation-disinflation-deflation

Marquand, B. (2024, May 3). *Government home loans to buy, refinance or renovate.* NerdWallet. *https://www.nerdwallet.com/article/mortgages/government-home-loans*

Marquand, B. (2024, May 9). *Mortgage closing costs: How much you'll pay.* NerdWallet. *https://www.nerdwallet.com/article/mortgages/closing-costs-mortgage-fees-explained*

Marquit, M. (n.d.). *5 Types Of Mortgage Loans For Homebuyers.* Bankrate. *https://www.bankrate.com/mortgages/types-of-mortgages/*

Martin, E. J. (2024, April 2). *Mortgage protection insurance (MPI) vs. life insurance.* Bankrate. *https://www.bankrate.com/mortgages/mortgage-protection-insurance-vs-life-insurance/#what-is*

Maverick, J. (2024, January 3). *S&P 500 Average Return and Historical Performance.* Investopedia. *https://www.investopedia.com/ask/answers/042415/what-average-annual-return-sp-500.asp*

Maverick, J. B. (2019). *What are some limitations of the consumer price index (CPI)?* Investopedia. *https://www.investopedia.com/ask/answers/012915/what-are-some-limitations-consumer-price-index-cpi.asp*

McCracken, R. (n.d.). *Here Are 10 Benefits of Owning a Home.* LendingTree. *https://www.lendingtree.com/home/mortgage/benefits-of-owning-home/*

Mckinsey & Company. (2022, August 17). *What Is inflation: the Causes and Impact.* Www.mckinsey.com. *https://www.mckinsey.com/featured-insights/mckinsey-explainers/what-is-inflation*

McMillin, D. (n.d.). *APR Vs. Interest Rate: What's The Difference?* Bankrate. *https://www.bankrate.com/mortgages/apr-and-interest-rate/*

McMillin, D. (n.d.). *Mortgage Rate Lock: What It Is And When To*

Lock. Bankrate. Retrieved February 16, 2024, from https://www.bankrate.com/mortgages/what-is-mortgage-rate-lock

Michael, G. (n.d.). The Dangers Of Deflation. Investopedia. https://www.investopedia.com/financial-edge/0311/the-dangers-of-deflation.aspx

Morris, C. (2021, January 18). Does adding a credit card improve your credit score? Experian. https://www.experian.com/blogs/ask-experian/does-adding-a-credit-card-improve-your-credit-score/

Mortgage answers. (n.d.). Consumer Financial Protection Bureau. https://www.consumerfinance.gov/consumer-tools/mortgages/answers/key-terms/

Mortgage Application: What It Is, How It Works. (n.d.). Investopedia. https://www.investopedia.com/terms/m/mortgage-application.asp

Mortgage Calculator. (2019). Mortgagecalculator.org; Mortgage Calculator. https://www.mortgagecalculator.org/

Muller, C. (2023, June 13). 14 Helpful Tips for Maintaining a Good Credit Score | Money Under 30. Https://Www.moneyunder30.com/. https://www.moneyunder30.com/tips-for-maintaining-a-good-credit-score/

Musinski, B. (2024, January 17). 5 tips to choose a mortgage lender. Forbes Advisor. https://www.forbes.com/advisor/mortgages/how-to-choose-a-mortgage-lender/

New Economics Foundation. (2020, January 27). Where does money come from? https://neweconomics.org/2012/12/where-does-money-come-from

Nmls, B. M. C. H. S. (2024, April 10). USDA Loan vs VA Loan: Rates, Eligibility, and More. Veterans United Network. https://www.veteransunited.com/education/va-loans-vs-usda-loans/

Number of Netflix paid subscribers by type 2018 | Statista. (2018). Statista; Statista. https://www.statista.com/statistics/258321/number-

of-netflix-subscribers-by-type/

Ostrowski, J. (2024, February 1). How to get rid of private mortgage insurance (PMI). Bankrate. https://www.bankrate.com/mortgages/removing-private-mortgage-insurance/

Payday Loan| Consumer Financial Protection Bureau. (2022, January 17). Consumer Financial Protection Bureau. https://www.consumerfinance.gov/ask-cfpb/what-is-a-payday-loan-en-1567/

Personal Saving rate. (2024, May 31). https://fred.stlouisfed.org/series/PSAVERT#0

Peter Drucker quotes. (n.d.). BrainyQuote. https://www.brainyquote.com/quotes/peter_drucker_131600

Pettinger, T. (2020, February 3). Economic effect of a devaluation of the currency. Economics Help. https://www.economicshelp.org/macroeconomics/exchangerate/effects-devaluation/

Poindexter, R. (2022, July 3). Did stimulus checks cause inflation? GOBankingRates. https://www.gobankingrates.com/money/economy/effect-stimulus-checks-on-inflation-overall-economy/

Real Estate Investment Trusts (REITs) | Investor.gov. (n.d.). https://www.investor.gov/introduction-investing/investing-basics/investment-products/real-estate-investment-trusts-reits

Recent trends in commercial bank balance sheets, Part 2 | FRED Blog. (n.d.). https://fredblog.stlouisfed.org/2023/04/recent-trends-in-commercial-bank-balance-sheets-part-2/

Reiff, N. (2023, July 31). Howey Test Definition: What it means and implications for cryptocurrency. Investopedia. https://www.investopedia.com/terms/h/howey-test.asp

Relationship Between Inflation, Gold, and Other Precious Metals. (2019, September 15). Provident Metals. https://www.providentmetals.com/knowledge-center/precious-metals-resources/inflation-precious-metals.html

Robert Kiyosaki Quotes. (n.d.). BrainyQuote. https://www.brainyquote.com/authors/robert-kiyosaki-quotes

Rollover old 401(k)s into IRAs with Schwab. (n.d.). Schwab Brokerage. https://www.schwab.com/ira/rollover-ira

Ross, S. (2023, December 19). Understanding how the Federal Reserve creates money. Investopedia. https://www.investopedia.com/articles/investing/081415/understanding -how-federal-reserve-creates-money.asp

Safe and Liquid Options for Your Emergency Fund. (n.d.). Investopedia. https://www.investopedia.com/ask/answers/13/safe-liquid-investment-for-emergencies.asp

Santarelli, M. (2023, April 1). Housing Market Crash 2008 Explained: Causes & Effects. Norada Real Estate Investments. https://www.noradarealestate.com/blog/housing-market-crash-2008/

SBA Loans: What You Need to Know. (n.d.). NerdWallet. https://www.nerdwallet.com/article/small-business/small-business-loans-sba-loans

SEC.gov | What are the differences in an IPO, a SPAC, and a direct listing? (2022, March 26). https://www.sec.gov/education/capitalraising/building-blocks/registered-offerings

Sharma, D. (2024, June 14). The Federal Reserve: Role, Functions, and Impact (2024 Guide). https://www.marketwatch.com/guides/banking/what-is-the-federal-reserve/

SIMPLE IRA plan. (n.d.). https://www.irs.gov/retirement-plans/plan-

sponsor/simple-ira-plan

Smith, L. (2022, January 31). *Inflation and deflation: Keep your portfolio safe. Investopedia.* https://www.investopedia.com/articles/basics/11/guarding-against-inflation-deflation.asp

SPY Stock Historical. Retrieved February 16, 2024, from https://finance.yahoo.com/quote/SPY/history?period1=946684800&period2=1702080000&interval=1mo&filter=history&frequency=1mo&includeAdjustedClose=true

Stalnaker, T., Usman, K., Buchanan, A., Alport, G., & Heilakka, R. (n.d.). *Airline Economic Analysis 2020 - 2021. Oliver Wyman.* https://www.oliverwyman.com/our-expertise/insights/2021/mar/airline-economic-analysis-2020-2021.html

Stevens, R. (2023, November 24). *How to calculate home appreciation - simple guide. New Silver.* https://newsilver.com/the-lender/how-to-calculate-home-appreciation/

Tackling Wage Inflation Within Healthcare. (2023, March 7). Www.shiftmed.com. https://www.shiftmed.com/blog/tackling-wage-inflation-within-healthcare/

Taylor, T. (2022, January 18). *Preparing for deflation? 10 tips to protect your finances - Starship. Starship.* https://www.starshiphsa.com/articles/preparing-for-deflation-10-tips-to-protect-your-finances/

Team, C. (2024, March 5). *Deflation. Corporate Finance Institute.* https://corporatefinanceinstitute.com/resources/economics/deflation/

Team, E. (2023, September 18). *Housing recessions and recoveries. CoreLogic®.* https://www.corelogic.com/intelligence/housing-recessions-and-recoveries/

Team, I. (2022, June 22). *Comprehensive Guide to Renters Insurance. Investopedia.* https://www.investopedia.com/insurance/renters-

insurance/

Team, I. (2023, December 17). *5 things you shouldn't do during a Recession. Investopedia.* https://www.investopedia.com/articles/pf/09/avoid-five-recession-risks.asp

Team, I. (2024, May 9). *What is economic growth and how is it measured? Investopedia.* https://www.investopedia.com/terms/e/economicgrowth.asp

Team, W. (2024, April 30). *Demand-Pull inflation. WallStreetMojo.* https://www.wallstreetmojo.com/demand-pull-inflation/#h-examples

The cost of homeownership vs. renting over 3, 5 and 10 years. (2019, January 26). *Mortgage Rates, Mortgage News and Strategy : The Mortgage Reports.* https://themortgagereports.com/46632/the-cost-of-homeownership-vs-renting-over-3-5-and-10-years

The Credit Score Needed to Buy a House. (n.d.). *NerdWallet.* https://www.nerdwallet.com/article/mortgages/whats-exact-credit-score-need-buy-home

The federal budget process | USAGov. (n.d.). https://www.usa.gov/federal-budget-process

The Federal Reserve Board. (2010). *The Federal Reserve's new rules for credit card companies. In www.federalreserve.gov.* https://www.federalreserve.gov/consumerinfo/wyntk/wyntk_ccrules.pdf

The Federal Reserve System Affects You More Than You Might Think. (2019). *Investopedia.* https://www.investopedia.com/articles/investing/090514/federal-reserve-system-affects-you-more-you-might-think.asp

The Great Recession | Federal Reserve History. (n.d.). *Www.federalreservehistory.org.* https://www.federalreservehistory.org/essays/great-recession-of-200709

References

The Investopedia Team. (2019). Deflation. Investopedia. https://www.investopedia.com/terms/d/deflation.asp

The Investopedia Team. (2019). Why Is Deflation Bad for the Economy? Investopedia. https://www.investopedia.com/articles/personal-finance/030915/why-deflation-bad-economy.asp

The long shadow of the 2001 recession | Federal Reserve Bank of Minneapolis. (n.d.). https://www.minneapolisfed.org/article/2023/the-long-shadow-of-the-2001-recession

Treasury bills in depth — TreasuryDirect. (n.d.). https://www.treasurydirect.gov/research-center/history-of-marketable-securities/bills/t-bills-indepth/

Treasury Bonds — TreasuryDirect. (n.d.). https://www.treasurydirect.gov/marketable-securities/treasury-bonds

Treasury Notes — TreasuryDirect. (n.d.). https://www.treasurydirect.gov/marketable-securities/treasury-notes/

U.S. Bureau of Labor Statistics. (2023). U.S. Bureau of Labor Statistics. Bls.gov; U.S. Bureau of Labor Statistics. https://data.bls.gov/pdq/SurveyOutputServlet

U.S. Inflation Calculator. (n.d.). U.S. Inflation Calculator. http://www.usinflationcalculator.com/

U.S. Treasury Securities | Vanguard. (n.d.). https://investor.vanguard.com/investor-resources-education/understanding-investment-types/us-treasury-bonds

Understand Your Credit Card Statement | MyCreditUnion.gov. (n.d.). Mycreditunion.gov. https://mycreditunion.gov/life-events/checking-credit-cards/credit-cards/statement

United States Joint Economic Committee. (2021, October 6). The economics of inflation and the risks of ballooning government spending. The Economics of Inflation and the Risks of Ballooning

References

Government Spending - United States Joint Economic Committee.
https://www.jec.senate.gov/public/index.cfm/republicans/2021/10/the-economics-of-inflation-and-the-risks-of-ballooning-government-spending

University of Illinois Chicago. (n.d.). https://publichealth.uic.edu/news-stories/study-finds-healthcare-sector-largely-immune-to-economic-downswings/

Vanguard. (2023). What's a bond? | Vanguard. Investor.vanguard.com.
https://investor.vanguard.com/investor-resources-education/understanding-investment-types/what-is-a-bond

Wage growth has been dampening inflation all along—and has slowed even more recently. (n.d.). Economic Policy Institute.
https://www.epi.org/blog/wage-growth-has-been-dampening-inflation-all-along-and-has-slowed-even-more-recently/

Webber, M. (2020). What is a Payday Loan? Investopedia.
https://www.investopedia.com/terms/p/payday-loans.asp

WEBBER, M. R. (2022, May 24). The Mortgage Process Explained.
Investopedia. https://www.investopedia.com/mortgage-process-explained-5213694

What does debt-to-income ratio mean & why is it important? | Chase.
(n.d.). Www.chase.com. https://www.chase.com/personal/credit-cards/education/basics/what-is-debt-to-income-ratio-and-why-it-is-important

What Happens During the Loan Application Process? (n.d.).
Resources.liveoakbank.com.
https://resources.liveoakbank.com/blog/what-happens-during-the-loan-application-process

What is a Security? (n.d.).
https://www.tn.gov/commerce/securities/investors/what-is-a-security.html

References

What Is An Escrow Account & How Do They Work | U.S. Bank. (n.d.). Www.usbank.com. https://www.usbank.com/home-loans/mortgage/first-time-home-buyers/what-is-an-escrow-account.html

What is an Excellent Credit Score? | Equifax. (n.d.). Www.equifax.com. https://www.equifax.com/personal/education/debt-management/articles/-/learn/credit-utilization-ratio/

What is financial news? (n.d.). Dow Jones Professional. Retrieved February 16, 2024, from https://www.dowjones.com/professional/glossary/what-is-financial-news/

What Is The Federal Reserve, In Plain English? (n.d.). Www.stlouisfed.org. https://www.stlouisfed.org/in-plain-english

Who measures GDP. (n.d.). https://www.bea.gov/sites/default/files/2018-04/GDP-Education-by-BEA.pdf

Wikipedia Contributors. (2019, February 1). Great Depression in the United States. Wikipedia; Wikimedia Foundation. https://en.wikipedia.org/wiki/Great_Depression_in_the_United_States

Young, J. (2023, December 17). Special Purpose Acquisition Company (SPAC) explained: Examples and risks. Investopedia. https://www.investopedia.com/terms/s/spac.asp

Made in United States
Troutdale, OR
11/17/2024

24954289R00076